THE GUERRILLA IS LIKE A POET.

this work is licensed under the creative commons
attribution-noncommercial-noderivs 3.0 unported license.
http://creativecommons.org/licenses/by-nc-nd/3.0/

printed by lightning source, milton keynes
in an endless edition (version 130927)
ISBN 978-90-817091-8-7

uitgeverij, den haag
shtëpia botuese, tiranë


www.uitgeverij.cc

JOSE MARIA SISON,

# The Guerrilla Is Like a Poet.

༄

# Ang Gerilya Ay Tulad ng Makata.

FOREWORD BY
JONAS STAAL.

⁞

Foreword –
The Cultural Worker as the
Guerrilla of the Stateless State

1.

As the founder of the New World Summit (NWS) and the New World Academy (NWA), I first of all would like to thank Professor Jose Maria Sison for participating as a speaker and teacher in our projects, and philosopher and publisher Vincent W.J. van Gerven Oei for his great involvement as advisor and chairman in the development of our summits, as well as for his willingness to publish this extensive survey of poetry by the founder of the Communist Party of the Philippines (CPP) and its armed wing, the New People's Army (NPA).

The New World Summit develops, through artistic means, "alternative parliaments" for organizations that currently find themselves excluded from democratic processes, for example by use of "designated lists of terrorist organizations." As such we facilitated Professor Sison as well as his colleague, Luis Jalandoni, on behalf of their organizations, CPP and NPA, as well as their negotiating body, the National Democratic Front of the Philippines (NDFP), who have all dealt with the effects of this type of legislation. Based in contemporary art center BAK in Utrecht, The New World Summit Academy for Cultural Activism, connects, in line with the New World Summit, artists and art students with organizations from the NWS network to collaborate on collective projects. These include the banned organizations themselves, as well as progressive political parties, diplomatic bodies, and other initiatives that oppose the current oppressive policies of what philosopher Alain Badiou has effectively named "capitalist democracy," or what I have consistently referred to as "democratism." Professor Sison, Luis Jalandoni, as well as the publisher of this book are all participating teachers in this academy.

The central question for these different organizations is how to situate the role of art in everyday political struggle. Through the New World Summit we explore the extent to which art can provide a political platform for unjustly banned organizations: where politics fails to act consequently upon the premise of a principled, fundamental democracy, we artists take over. As such we defend art as "more political than politics itself," facilitating voices beyond the limits of democratism. Through the New World Academy we investigate how banned organizations and their progressive allies have deployed art in everyday political practice. As such, NWS proposes an alternative infrastructure to think of the role of art in the realm of progressive political movements.

Within the current doctrine of democratism art is subjected to what Theodor Adorno referred to as the "cultural industry," the friendly, civilized face of a system that imposes structural violence through (economic) colonization and exploitation as well as militarization in order to protect the privileged sphere of Western citizens, citizens who themselves have become part of a system of monitoring and control, to prevent them from ever attempting to expose or oppose the structural violence that is at the foundation of our current political order. In this context, art is nothing but a propagandistic tool for the political status quo: a perverted and regressive theater, whose fourth wall we refuse – or are too intimidated – to destroy. Our voting rounds serve what the Japanese, whose democratic system was imposed by the US after World War II, refer to as "democratism." The ideology of capitalist democracy focused on global monopolization under the guise of "liberation" and "human rights," rather than what we could refer to as a "fundamental democracy": democracy as an *emancipatory movement*.

Since the fall of the Berlin Wall democratism has become globally accepted as the political norm, as a condition that should be considered the "least of all evils." So-called totalitarianism ought to have taught the West the lesson no longer to strive for "utopian" politics, but to aim for consensus-based administration: a consensus between the free market and the state; a consensus between the stateless and the citizen; a consensus between the conservative right and the revolutionary left… Consensus where consensus is impossible, namely in the domain of emancipatory egalitarian politics. This consensus proposed to us at the supposed end of history is false. We are told that our dreams of a different world are utopian while the most dystopian global system of exploitation and repression ever devised is in place. We did not choose the least of all evils; we have come to accept the *worst one*. The cultural industry serves to provide a democratic appearance to a system unworthy of such name.

Now, in recent years, global political changes have become visible. The rise of the new economies – Brazil, Russia, China, and India – has made it evident that the old Empire is slowly being torn apart. That certainly does not mean that we are witnessing the rise of "more democratic states," but what is relevant is that substantial cracks are becoming apparent, showing the "end of the end of history," as new globally competing powers manifest themselves. These cracks are signs of unexpected subversions taking place within the discourse of democratism. Putin's choice to grant asylum to whistleblower Edward Snowden, who exposed the worldwide spying network of the US-based and EU-facilitated National Security Agency (NSA) and whom the US intends to put on trial for this "treason" would be one recent example. Now the real treason is the fact that states spy on their citizens, even though this is a reality that Putin – whose regime systematically marginalizes and suppresses minorities and possible "foreign agitators" – is hardly interested in. Putin's regime performs a power play under the guise of concern for democracy and Snowden's right to free speech. It is a power play that shows that the Western hegemony on democratist discourse is over, allowing new, minor players to start operating on their own terms, such as Ecuador which granted asylum to whistleblower Julian Assange. Ecuadorian president Rafael Correa is here the leading provocateur, offering the US "third world help" in the form of "human rights training for its administrators,"

Within these cracks other, non-statist practices are appearing as well: the Indignados protests in Spain, the worldwide Occupy Movement, and the Gezi Park protests in Turkey, many movements within what is roughly referred to as the Arab Spring, as well as the rise of the new democratic digitalization movement in the shape of the international Pirate Parties and Wikileaks. These movements operate between parliamentary and non-parliamentary action, demanding more than the state could ever offer: the democratization of our politics, of our economy, and our ecology. Not through yet another round of voting, but by breaking the monopolies of power engineered by the democratist state, and by providing the people with the democratic tools necessary to shape their own lives and communities. This is what I refer to as a movement in defense of a *fundamental democracy*. This is a concept irreconcilable with democratism.

So we are faced by a choice, between democratism and fundamental democracy. It is a choice for two different notions of politics, two different notions of culture. Two different notions of *art*.

2.
What is today considered the national democratic movement of the Philippines consists of a variety of underground movements as well as (semi)legal political parties and organizations with a strong leftist, Maoist signature. Its historic base is nonetheless to be found in the revolutionary figure of Andrés Bonifacio (1863–1897), who demanded Filipino independence from the Spanish colonialists that had occupied the country since the 16th century. Backed by the American promise of an independent Filipino republic, Emilio Aguinaldo led the Filipino resistance forces in 1898 during the Spanish–American War. The United States however did not keep its promise, and occupied the country until 1946 after which it continued to

instrumentalize its "independent" governments. The national democratic movement movement gained its strength in the period of the US-backed Marcos dictatorship, from 1965 to 1986, when the Communist Party of the Philippines (founded in 1968) and its armed wing, the New People's Party (founded in 1969) gained strength by mobilizing the peasant and worker population through guerrilla struggle. The Vietnam War fueled the anger against the continuous colonial policies of the Americans who, despite the formal independence of the Philippines in 1946, continued to control the country by supporting puppet regimes.

It was around 1960 that Professor Sison joined the call of Senator Claro Mayo Recto for a "second propaganda movement," a cultural uprising demanding independence. The first propaganda movement had manifested itself against the Spanish under the leadership of nationalists and former writers and journalists, among whom Jose Rizal, Marcelo H. del Pilar, and Graciano Lopez Jaena were the central figures, and this second movement was to be employed against the Marcos regime and its foreign backing. It is in this context that the figure of the artist as *cultural worker* emerged, a figure central to understanding the role of art within the national democratic movement in general and the present book of Sison's collected poetry in particular. The cultural worker still exists today against the background of an ongoing guerrilla struggle in defense of landless peasants and the urban poor, who, according to the National Democratic Movement, continue to be deprived of their right to self-determination; after the Marcos dictatorship, subsequent governments have continued to sell off land to foreign investors and their private militias, characterizing Filipino politics, in Sison's words, as a "semi-colonial and semi-feudal ruling system under US imperialist control" and with the "comprador big bourgeoisie, landlords and bureaucrat capitalists" as the ruling classes.

Professor Sison has been at the forefront of the resistance by founding the main party and defense forces of the movement, working alongside the guerrillas until his capture by Marcos's forces in 1977. He was subsequently imprisoned and tortured over a period of nine years. He was released in 1986, when president Corazon Aquino, the wife of Benigno Aquino – a murdered opponent of the dictatorship – had become the face of the massive uprising against the regime, even though the military strongly objected to setting the rebel leader free. Sison opposed the Aquino government after his release for continuing the oppression of the peasant population and lacking in the necessary reform that would allow the Philippines to develop to full independence from US influence. As a result, his return to the Philippines was obstructed by Aquino by canceling his passport while on a lecture tour in 1988, forcing him to seek exile in the Netherlands, where he has remained ever since.

In exile he has continued to be the intellectual frontliner of the Filipino national democratic movement, and battle the United States which, in the aftermath of September 11, 2001, placed him on a list of terrorist suspects – a decision in which the European Union followed suit, but which was overturned with help of lawyer Jan Fermon. As such, Professor Sison is not only a leading figure in the national democratic movement of the Philippines, but also embodies and enacts himself, in his position of exile, the consequences of the so-called "War On Terror": a global war not against so-called terrorists, but against citizens, leading to a massive erosion of civil rights worldwide and a de facto permanent declaration of "martial law." Marcos's declaration of the "state of emergency" in the Philippines in 1972 in order to fight a military and extrajudicial war against the Communist uprisings in the country; the state of emergency declared by President George W. Bush after the attacks of September 11, 2001, allowing for massive policing of citizens through its NSA; the extrajudicial prisons of Abu Ghraib and Guantánamo and its overall lobby to kill and extradite non-US citizens worldwide for military trial – history repeats itself perversely. Sison lived, opposed and was subjected to these never ending policies of the state of emergency.

In the face of the state of emergency, the second propaganda movement declares the cultural worker to be the figure embodying the Filipino people's right to self-determination, continuing to inscribe through his or her words and images the collective symbolic universe that would otherwise have been an independent state. The artist is a cultural worker. He or she uses the tool of art in order to uphold the narratives and convictions of those marginalized, dispossessed, and persecuted through the dark depths of the militarized state. He or she is educator, agitator, organizer – all in order to maintain and continue to enact, to *perform*, the symbolic universe of the unacknowledged state – not so much an administrative entity but rather as a *collective condition*. As such the long cultural struggle of the Filipino people has created a state in itself, a detailed network of references, histories, symbols, that define a people's identity *far beyond what a state could ever contain.* It is within this stateless state that we find the condition that may be understood as a "permanent revolution," that is, the permanent process of collectively inscribing, criticizing, contesting, and altering our understanding of communal culture. Not as administered identities, but as identities in permanent revolt against the conditions that define our everyday struggle. This does not mean that culture can somehow abolish the state, but that if there should ever be such a thing as a state, it should be an instrument of this permanent process in which a *people's culture* manifests itself, and not an administrative entity regulating it.

It is in this line of argument that the guerrilla appears in Sison's work, and as the main title of these collected works. The ultimate cultural worker *cannot be but a poet.* As a consequence, the process in which a stateless people organizes and struggles to articulate and defend its commons, cannot be anything else but a *total work of art* – a *Gesamtkunstwerk*. The people are not simply artists; they are *the work of art in themselves.* The cultural worker is the guerrilla of this stateless state of a common culture, praising and singing the process in which the total work of art – the people – manifests itself constantly.

3.
In this foreword I have introduced two narratives. The first is that of today's international democratization movement reaching from the Indignados protests in Spain to the Gezi Park revolts in Turkey which the New World Summit and Academy

believe to comprise the potential international mass base that will define the future of the project of a fundamental democracy. The second is that of the national democratic movement in which Sison has played and continues to play a crucial role, reaching from the early revolt of Andrés Bonifacio against the Spanish occupation to the anti-colonialist rise of the militant left against the US occupation, and whose stateless state of a common culture is currently upheld by generations of cultural workers in the Philippines.

I do not claim that the National Democratic Movement and the international democratization movement can be conflated, but they certainly share a common opponent in the form of a monopolized global condition of democratism. The generations of cultural workers can teach the international democratization movement that art is no mere luxury or artifact in our state museums. It is a weapon with which we pull down the propaganda of the status-quo so as to confront and change the concrete conditions of the world we inhabit.

This book with the collected work of Professor Sison – a guerrilla of the stateless state – will contribute to upholding this progressive truth.

– Jonas Staal

Preface

I am delighted and honored that my book of poems, *The Guerrilla Is Like a Poet,* is published in connection with the project of the Academy for Cultural Activism to present to artists and students in The Netherlands the role of art and literature in the struggle of the Filipino people for national liberation and democracy.

I thank Jonas Staal of the Academy for Cultural Activism and Dr. Vincent van Gerven Oei of Uitgeverij for asking me to make the selection of poems, juxtapose the Pilipino and English versions and include commentaries that shed light on the significance, content and style of the poems and on my track record in the new democratic revolution of my people and the place that I have earned in Philippine literature.

I have divided the poems into three parts. The first part is titled "The People's Resistance" and the poems are about the revolutionary struggle of the toiling masses against their foreign and feudal oppressors. The second part is titled "Detention and Defiance" and the poems are about my torture and imprisonment by the Marcos fascist dictatorship from 1977 to 1986. The third part is titled "The Struggle Continues" and the poems are about the perseverance of the Filipino people and myself in struggle.

The poems in the first and second part are selected from my book of poems, *Prison and Beyond,* which won the Southeast Asia WRITE Award for poetry in 1986 and which carries the poem, "The Guerrilla Is Like a Poet." The third part of the present book includes poems that I have written while in exile as a political refugee in the Netherlands.

These more recent poems reflect the continuous suffering and struggle of the Filipino people, the depredations of the imperialist policy of neoliberalism, my work for international solidarity along the anti-imperialist and democratic line as Chairperson of the International League of Peoples' Struggle and my subjection to "terrorist" blacklisting initiated by the US government and to arrest and solitary confinement by the Dutch government on false charges of murder by the Philippine government.

In dovetailing the Pilipino and English versions of the poems, I was advised and assisted by J. Luneta, Cora Mercado and Julie de Lima who are experts in the two languages. I made the final decision on variations or differences of translation. I am therefore totally responsible for the texts.

In this preface, I say just enough to open the door and welcome your reading of the poems. I hope that you understand and appreciate how I try to express within the brevity of poems, so much thought and feeling, which I would have otherwise expressed in volumes of prose.

I have included in the book as fourth part a brief statement of mine on the literary craft and commitment and the commentaries on my poetry by Filipino colleagues who are renowned in the Philippines and abroad as teachers of literature, literary critics and practising poets. For the commentaries and appreciation for my poetry, I thank Prof. E. San Juan, Jr., Dr.

Elmer Ordoñez, Prof. Bien Lumbrera, the late Petronilo Bn. Daroy, the late Alfredo Salanga, Gelacio Guillermo, Nonilon Queaño, Luis V. Teodoro and Edgar Maranan.

I take this opportunity to express my admiration and gratitude to Jonas Staal and all his colleagues in the New World Summit (NWS) for having provided democratic space to the Filipino people's struggle for national liberation and democracy. I appreciate the artistic way that NWS creates the architectural venue for the alternative parliament and for the expression of ideas excluded by those who wield power and amass private wealth.

In the First New World Summit in Berlin in 2011, the National Democratic Front of the Philippines (NDFP) was featured as one of the major national liberation movements in the world. Luis Jalandoni had ample opportunity to present the revolutionary mission and vision of the NDFP.

In the Second New World Summit in Leiden in 2012, I was given the privilege of being the main speaker to articulate the Filipino people's democratic program and struggle for national and social liberation, to express my grievance against the "terrorist" blacklisting and to expound on the NDFP desire for a just and lasting peace in pursuing peace negotiations with the Manila government.

I am elated that the NWS and its founder Jonas Staal have proceeded to create the Academy for Cultural Activism. I believe that this endeavor will encourage artists and teachers of art to imbue their work with the revolutionary spirit and carry forward the necessary progressive and fruitful dialectical relationship of art and democratization towards a new and better world of greater freedom, social justice, all-round development and international solidarity of the people.

– Jose Maria Sison, 1 September 2013

*first part · the people's resistance*

*unang bahagi · ang paglaban ng sambayanan*

## The Guerrilla Is Like a Poet

The guerrilla is like a poet
Keen to the rustle of leaves
The break of twigs
The ripples of the river
The smell of fire
And the ashes of departure.

The guerrilla is like a poet.
He has merged with the trees
The bushes and the rocks
Ambiguous but precise
Well-versed on the law of motion
And master of myriad images.

The guerrilla is like a poet.
Enrhymed with nature
The subtle rhythm of the greenery
The inner silence, the outer innocence
The steel tensile in-grace
That ensnares the enemy.

The guerrilla is like a poet.
He moves with the green brown multitude
In bush burning with red flowers

## Ang Gerilya Ay Tulad ng Makata

Ang gerilya ay tulad ng makata
Matalas sa kaluskos ng mga dahon
Sa pagkabali ng mga sanga
Sa mga onda ng ilog
Sa amoy ng apoy
At sa abo ng paglisan.

Ang gerilya ay tulad ng makata
Nakasanib sa mga puno
Sa mga palumpong at rokas
Nakakaalangan subalit tumpak
Bihasa sa batas ng paggalaw
Pantas sa laksang larawan.

Ang gerilya ay tulad ng makata
Karima ng kalikasan
Ng sutlang ritmo ng kaluntian
Katahimikang panloob, kamusmusang panlabas
Aserong tibay ng panatag na loob
Na sumisilo sa kaaway.

Ang gerilya ay tulad ng makata
Kasabay ng luntiang, kayumangging masa
Sa palumpong na pinaliliyab ng mga pulang bulaklak

That crown and hearten all
Swarming the terrain as a flood
Marching at last against the stronghold.

An endless movement of strength
Behold the protracted theme:
The people's epic, the people's war.

*1968*

Na nagkokorona at nagpapaalab sa lahat,
Dumadagsa sa kalupaan tulad ng baha
Nagmamartsa sa wakas laban sa kuta.

Walang hanggang daloy ng lakas,
Masdan ang matagalang tema
Ng epikong bayan, ng digmang bayan.

*1968*

## The Bladed Poem

Behold the bladed poem
Tensile and razor-sharp
Cold and glinting silver
In the light or dark.

See how the blackbird
Of a hilt flies
Bedecked with pearls
On the firm mobile hand.

Look at each face
On the leaf of steel,
The virile subtle flames,
Images of incised gold.

On one face are toilers
Varied with pike and ore,
Crucible, hammer and anvil,
Water and whetstone.

Plow and carabao on soil,
The oyster in the sea,
Carving and etching tools,
Bowl of acid on a table.

## Ang Tulang may Talim

Masdan ang tulang may talim
Matibay at sintalas ng labaha
Malamig at kumikinang na pilak
Sa liwanag o sa dilim.

Tingnan kung paano lumilipad
Ang ibong-itim na puluhang
Pinaganda ng mga perlas
Sa matatag at maliksing kamay.

Suriin ang bawat mukha
Sa dahong asero,
Ang mga matipuno't pinong liyab,
Mga iniukit na gintong larawan.

Sa isang mukha'y mga anakpawis,
Sari-saring may piko at mineral,
Pugon, martilyo at pandayan,
Tubig at batong hasaan.

Araro at kalabaw sa lupa,
Mga talaba sa dagat,
Mga gamit panlilok at pang-ukit,
Mangkok ng asido sa mesa.

On the other face
Are the same workmen massed
Upright and poised to fight
Behind the radiant flag.

The uprising completes
The figures of labor
And urges another surge
With the well-versed weapon.

Grasp well the bladed poem
And let it sing in your hands.
This kampilan is a talisman
Of the people in red headbands.

*1 March 1982*

Sa kabilang mukha
Ang mga anakpawis pa ring nakatipon
Nakatindig at handang lumaban
Sa likod ng nagniningning na watawat.

Linulubos ng pagbalikwas
Ang mga anyo ng paggawa
At inuudyok ang bagong pagsulong,
Taglay ang matatas na sandata.

Tanganan ang tulang may talim
At paawitin sa inyong mga kamay.
Ang kampilang ito ay agimat
Ng mga mamamayang may potong na pula.

*1 Marso 1982*

## The Woman and the Strange Eagle

The sea roars mightily around us,
Urging us to let a new life bud.
The woman on our boat is in travail,
Our vigorous rowing must be of avail.
We can ride on the giant waves.

Yet a strange eagle shuts out the sun.
Its talons of steel drip with blood;
Its wings stir the wind and darken the skies;
It has diamantine devouring eyes;
Shreds of flesh are in its razor blade.

But look, it has a wound of its own.
Hurry up, aim the sharpened arrow
And bend our strong narra bow.
We despise the eagle's accursed shadow
Cast on the woman and the boat.

We shall not drift in darkness.
We know our seas and islands well.
Our will is firm and we know the way.
We can prevail against this bird of prey.
As our neighbors have done in the fray.

## Ang Babae at ang Dayong Agila

Kaylakas ng ugong ng dagat sa paligid,
Nang-uudyok na paluwalin ang bagong buhay.
Naghihirap manganak ang babae sa ating bangka,
Dapat makatulong ang malakas na paggaod.
Masasakyan natin ang mga dambuhalang alon.

Subalit tinatakpan ng dayong agila ang araw.
Tumutulo ng dugo ang mga aserong kuko;
Mga pakpak, ginugulo ang hangi't pinadidilim ang langit;
May dyamantinang mga matang sumisila;
Gutay-gutay na mga laman sa matalim na tuka.

Ngunit masdan, may angking sugat ito.
Dali, isipat ang pinatulis na palaso
At banatin ang malakas na busog narra.
Suklam tayo sa kasumpa-sumpang anino ng agila
Na lumulukob sa babae at sa bangka.

Hindi tayo maaanod sa kadiliman.
Gamay natin ang mga dagat at isla.
Matatag ang ating loob at alam natin ang daan.
Mananaig tayo sa ibong mandaragit
Tulad ng ginawa ng mga karatig-bayan sa pakikibaka.

The landward east wind is in our favor;
We cannot get lost in our labor.
Look at how the red sail is blown
And how the red lamp glows in gathering storm.
We shall surely reach our port.

The child of darkness and the tempest,
The child of this suffering woman,
Shall be born in a strong house
Well-lighted and firm in the ground.
Her pangs shall be her joy without bonds.

From the rockspring, we shall fetch
Water that is purest and sweetest
To bathe the child and slake the mother's thirst
We shall give her honey and fruits
So her milk shall be rich and abundant.

In the brightness of day, we shall gather
The reddest of roses and all fragrant flowers
And fill the natal room with them.
It shall be a day we can never forget.
A joyous day of victory for all our kindred.

*5 March 1978*

Kapanig natin ang silangang hanging padalampasigan;
Hindi tayo maliligaw sa ating pagpapagod.
Masdan paano hipan ng hangin ang pulang layag
At ang liyab ng pulang lampara sa nagbabadyang unos.
Tiyak tayong aabot sa ating daungan.

Ang anak ng dilim at sigwa,
Ang anak ng babaeng naghihirap
Ay isisilang sa bahay na matibay
Maaliwalas at matatag sa lupa.
Hapdi'y magiging ligayang walang hanggan.

Mula sa batis na bukal ng bato iigib tayo
Ng tubig na pinakadalisay at pinakamatamis
Upang paliguan ang sanggol at pawiin ang uhaw ng ina.
Hahainan natin siya ng pulot at prutas
Na pampayama't pampasagana ng kanyang ng gatas.

Sa liwanag ng araw, mamumupol tayo
Ng pinakapulang rosas at lahat ng mabangong bulaklak
At pupunuin nitong alay ang silid na sinilangan.
Magiging araw itong hindi natin malilimutan kailanman.
Maligayang araw ng tagumpay para sa tanang kaangkan.

*5 Marso 1978*

## Against the Monster on the Land

For centuries the monster on the land
Has gorged himself on flesh and blood.
Now he wields a brittle rusty sword
And still casts a spell with a cross.

We go with the children of wrath
And prepare a trap across his path:
A net of vine holding a carpet of leaves
Covers the pit full of bamboo spears.

When he stumbles into the hungry hole
And raves and writhes among the poles
He shall see the children of the soil
Casting upon him buckets of flaming oil.

The night shall flee from the flames.
These shall rage until the break of day
And merge with the glory of the sun.
The monster shall have been gone.

Laban sa Halimaw sa Lupa

Daan-daang taon nang nagpakasasa
Sa laman at dugo ang halimaw sa lupa.
Ngayon tangan ang espadang dupok sa kalawang
At gamit pa ang gayuma ng krus.

Sama tayo sa mga anak ng galit
At umangan ng bitag ang kanyang daan
Lambat na baging na binanigan ng mga dahon
Panakip sa hukay na siksik sa matutulis na kawayan.

Kapag nahulog siya sa gutom na hukay
At magsisigaw at mamilipit sa matutulis na tikin
Mapapatingala siya sa mga anak ng lupa
Na sa kanya'y balde-baldeng langis na umaapoy na ibinubuhos.

Tatakas ang gabi sa mga liyab,
Lalagablab hanggang bukang-liwayway
At sasanib sa luwalhati ng araw.
Pumanaw na noon ang halimaw.

His sword shall break by a hammer blow
On a rock from which a sweet spring flows.
The fragments of the sword we shall gather
To fashion new things by the hammer.

The children of the soil shall be freed
Of yoke and terror in their country.
They shall stand against any monster
And win by wit and engulfing number.

The festival of the children of the soil
Is the festival of all children of toil.
We joyously sing and dance with them
As the ancient monster comes to an end.

*17 March 1978*

Espada niya'y mababasag sa bayo ng maso
Sa malaking batong bukal ng matamis na batis.
Mga tatal ng espada'y ating titipunin
Upang mga bagong bagay sa maso'y hubugin.

Lalaya ang mga anak ng lupa
Sa singkaw at lagim sa sariling bayan.
Titindig sila laban sa anumang halimaw
At sa talino't panalikop na bilang ay magtatagumpay.

Ang pista ng mga anak ng lupa
Ay pista ng tanang anakpawis.
Sa kanila malugod tayong makiawit at makisayaw
Sa pagpanaw ng sinaunang halimaw.

*17 Marso 1978*

## The Forest Is Still Enchanted

The fickle-minded spirits and fairies
Have fled the old trees and bushes,
Dark caves and mounds in the shadows,
Mossy rocks and whispering streams.
The gnarled balete and the blackbird
Have lost their intriguing power.

The uncertainties of the past ages
No longer lurk to exact awe and fear.
In the forest throbs discreetly
A certainty above the certainties
Of chopping wood, hunting boar and deer,
Gathering fruits, honey and even orchids.

But the forest is still enchanted.
There is a new hymn in the wind;
There is a new magic in the dark green,
So the peasant folks say to friends.
A single fighting spirit has taken over
To lure in and astonish the intruders.

*June 1981*

## Nakakabighani Pa ang Gubat

Lumayas na ang sumpunging mga anito at diwata
Sa matatandang puno at palumpong,
Madidilim na yungib at puntod sa lilim,
Lumuting mga bato at bumubulong na mga sapa.
Ang pilipit na balete at ang uwak
Nawalan na ng kapangyarihang manindak.

Mga alinlangan ng sinaunang panahon
Ay hindi na nakaambang manggulat at manakot.
Mahinahong tumitibok sa gubat
Ang isang katiyakang nakaibabaw sa mga katiyakan
Ng pangangahoy, pangangaso ng baboy damo at usa,
Pamimitas ng mga prutas, pulot-pukyutan at orkidya.

Subalit nakakabighani pa ang gubat.
May bagong himig sa hangin;
May bagong hiwaga sa kulimlim na luntian,
Sabi ng mga magsasaka sa mga kaibigan.
Nananaig ang iisang mapanlabang diwa
Para umangan at gulantangin ang mga mapanghimasok.

*Hunyo 1981*

## Defy the Reptile

In the gloomy swamp of barbaric times
Fear creates a god in the crocodile
And plays on the innocent child
A nightmare of almighty jaws,
All-seeing eyes, limitless guile,
Adeptest claws and toughest hide.

Praises and offerings to the reptile
Whet the whining bloody appetite
And make the bamboo raft more fragile.
The scrubs around and above cast shadows
And the dark rocks below assume forms
To magnify, multiply the slithering terror.

But when the monster itself appears,
It reveals its limited size and puny parts.
The lonely person is roused to resist
And resorts to his knife and wile
To defy the reptile and old beliefs
And inspire more men to use their spears.

Labanan ang Buwaya

Sa mapanglaw na latian ng barbarikong panahon
Nililikha ng takot ang diyos sa buwaya.
At iniaamba sa walang-muwang na paslit
Ang bangungot sa labis na makapangyarihang panga,
Mga matang nakakakita ng lahat, katusuhang walang hanggan,
Pinakamaliksing pangalmot at pinakamatigas na balat.

Ang mga papuri't alay sa buwaya
Ay pampagana sa maungol na pagkahayok sa dugo
At lalong nagpaparupok sa kawayang balsa.
Mga sukal sa paligid at sa itaas ay lumilikha ng mga anino
At ang madidilim na bato sa ilalim ay nagkakaanyo
Upang palakihin, paramihin ang madulas na lagim.

Ngunit sa paglitaw mismo ng halimaw,
Inilalantad nito ang limitadong sukat at maliliit na bahagi.
Ang nag-iisang tao'y napupukaw nasumalungat
At gumamit ng tabak at lalang
Upang labanan ang buwaya't mga lumang paniniwala
At himukin ang mas marami pa na magsigamit ng sibat.

Folks learn to bait the beast with toads
And then to set upon its securest lair.
Thus, one crocodile god after another
Yields its teeth to the circle of spears.
And these become the amulets, tokens
Of proven willful strength of men.

*March 1982*

Natututo ang mga tao na painan ang hayop ng mga kabatsoy
At saka lusubin sa pinakaligtas nitong yungib.
Sa gayon, magkakasunod na buwayang diyos
Ang nagsisisuko ng pangil sa mga sibat na pumapalibot.
Mga ito'y nagiging agimat, mga sagisag
Ng napatunayang mapagpasiyang lakas ng tao.

*Marso 1982*

## The Central Plains

I love the green expanse of ricefields,
The sunlight that strikes it reveals
The myriads of golden beads.
I love the sturdy stand of the canefields,
The sunlight that strikes it reveals
The golden wands of sweetness.

The breeze sweeping the plains carries
The rhythm of toil of peasants and farm workers.
I love the clangor on the road and in shops
As workers make do with some machines.
I love the blue mountains yonder;
They evince hope to all the toilers.

   *15 August 1978*

## Ang Gitnang Kapatagan

Mahal ko ang luntiang lawak ng palayan,
Itinatambad ng sikat ng araw
Ang laksa-laksang ginintuang butil.
Mahal ko ang matikas na tindig ng tubuhan
Itinatambad ng sikat ng araw
Ang ginintuang mga baston ng katamisan.

Dala ng simoy na kumakalat sa kapatagan
Ang kumpas ng trabaho ng mga anakpawis.
Mahal ko ang ingay sa daan at pagawaan
Habang gamit ng mga manggagawa ang ilang makina.
Mahal ko ang bughaw na mga bundok sa kalayuan
Nagpapahiwatig ng pag-asa sa lahat ng anakpawis.

*15 Agosto 1978*

From a Burning Bush

The voice of the people thunders forth
From a burning bush in the mountain,
Unite to overthrow the rule of terror
And the three gods of exploitation.

The lightning tongue of the fiery bush
Crackles and carries the flames
Over the rolling hills and meadows
To the expectant valleys and plains.

More burning bushes rage and roar,
Boldly break out into fields of flames
And send up high flying scrolls
From the fields of stubble that blaze.

Lightnings smite the tower of idols.
The flying scrolls enter the apertures
And invite the flames from the stubble
To close in on the roots of the tower.

*15 July 1978*

## Mula sa Umaapoy na Palumpong

Dumadagundong ang tinig ng bayan
Mula sa umaapoy na palumpong sa bundok,
Magkaisa't ibagsak ang paghahari ng lagim
At ang tatlong diyos ng pagsasamantala.

Ang dilang kidlat ng malagablab na palumpong
Lumalagutok at nagdadala ng mga liyab
Sa umaalong mga burol at kaparangan
Hanggang sa sabik na mga lambak at kapatagan.

Dagdag pang mga palumpong na lumalagablab
Ang matapang na umaalpas na maging larangang apoy
At nagpapalipad pataas ng mga kasulatan
Mula sa mga tuyot na parang na lumiliyab.

Mga kidlat ang gumagahis sa tore ng mga diyos-diyosan.
Ang kasulatang lumilipad, sumusuot sa mga siwang
At nag-aanyaya ng mga liyab mula sa kaparangan
Upang ang tore mula sa ugat ay salikupan.

*15 Hulyo 1978*

## The Coming of the Rain

Gathered by the oppressive heat
Heavy clouds darken all beneath
But thunder and lightning proclaim
A new season of growth in the rain.

The wide wind and deepening stream
Race from the mountain to bring
The message in a more intimate way,
The coming of the rain to the plains.

The trees raise their arms to the sky
And dance in a movement so spright.
The bushes raise and blend their voices
With the trees in song and laughter.

The wind sweeps away the fallen leaves
And fans the spark on the stubbly field.
The flames leap and whet the thirst
Of the earth so eager for the water thrusts.

*15 June 1978*

## Ang Pagdating ng Ulan

Tinipon ng mapaniil na init
Pinadidilim ng makakapal na ulap ang lahat sa ilalim
Subalit ipinapahayag ng kulog at kidlat
Ang bagong panahon ng paglago sa ulan.

Ang malawak na hangin at papalalim na agos
Nag-uunahan mula bundok para dalhin
Ang mensahe sa mas matalik na paraan,
Ang pagdating ng ulan sa kapatagan.

Nagsisitaas ang mga punungkahoy ng mga bisig sa langit
At sumasayaw sa maliksing kadensa.
Mga halaman nagsisitaas at nagsisisaliw ng mga tinig nila
Sa mga punongkahoy sa awit at halakhak.

Itinataboy ng hangin ang mga lagas na dahon
At pinapaypayan ang titis sa tuyot na parang.
Lumulundag ang mga liyab at nagpapatindi ng uhaw
Ng lupang napakasabik sa tarak ng ulan.

*15 Hunyo 1978*

## Under the Rain

Behold the vast ocean of green blades
Linking and floating the villages.
What a great mastery of rain, sun and land
By the unschooled peasants.

Something more is within their power
Among them are the cadres and fighters.
They thrive together under the rain
In a fluid movement for new gains.

The villages are shrouded in mystery
The enemy finds the roads too slippery
And the foliage abets his blind fright.
The low evil birds of prey cannot fly.

It is the turn of the revolutionaries
To launch wise and brave sallies
While more comrades in a limitless rear
Merge with the masses in work and study.

*15 June 1973*

Sa Ulan

Masdan ang malawak na karagatan ng luntiang dahon
Nag-uugnay at nagpapalutang sa mga nayon.
Anong dakilang kapantasan sa ulan, araw at lupa
Ang sa mga magsasakang di nakatuntong sa paaralan.

Higit pa rito ang sakop ng kanilang kapangyarihan
Sa hanay nila ang mga kadre at mandirigma.
Sama-sama silang lumalago sa ulan
Sa kilusang madaloy tungong mga bagong tagumpay.

Nalalambungan ng hiwaga ang mga nayon.
Napakadulas ng mga daan para sa kaaway
At pinatitindi ng mga halaman ang bulag niyang takot.
Hindi makalipad ang mabababang imbing ibong mandaragit.

Pagkakataon na ng mga rebolusyonaryo
Na maglunsad ng matatalino at magigiting na daluhong
Habang mas maraming kasama sa likurang walang hangganan
Ay kasanib ng masa sa paggawa at pag-aaral.

*15 Hunyo 1973*

Rain and Sun on the Mountains

When thunder and lightning are over,
Cold dark clouds seem to dissolve
The mountains into an ugly murk.
But behind the dismal sight,
Rain soaks the earth, floats detritus
And pours life into the creeks and rivers,
Amidst the howling of the wind,
The trees and bushes at the heights
Are in deepgoing nourishment.
So are the crops on the plains.

Then the sun breaks out of the gloom
To give warmth to the mountains,
To keep the roots of the woods
More firm on the ground.
The green splendor of all foliage
Shines and is celebrated
By the wild singing of the birds
And the happy antics of the beast.
In the cool breeze, the sunlight shafts
The limpid thirst-quenching waters.

## Ulan at Araw sa Kabundukan

Paglipas ng kulog at kidlat
Wari'y nilulusaw ng malamig, madilim na mga ulap
Ang kabundukan tungong karimlan.
Subalit sa likod ng mapanglaw na tanawin,
Pinipigta ng ulan ang lupa, pinalulutang ang layak
At binubuhusan ng buhay ang mga sapa at ilog.
Sa pag-ugong ng hangin
Ang mga puno't halaman sa kaitaasan
Ay malalim na nagpapakabusog.
Gayundin ang mga pananim sa kapatagan.

Saka, humuhulagpos ang araw mula sa karimlan
Upang magdulot ng init sa kabundukan,
Panatilihin ang mga ugat ng mga gubat
Sa mahigpit na pagkabaon sa lupa.
Ang luntiang kariktan ng lahat ng halaman
Ay kumikinang at ipinagdiriwang
Ng napakasiglang kantahan ng mga ibon
At masayang kantihan ng mga hayop.
Sa maginhawang simoy ng hangin, tinatagos ng araw
Ang malinaw, pantighaw-uhaw na tubig ng batis.

If there were only rain and storm,
The mountains would turn into mud.
If there were only sun and drought,
The mountains would turn into dust.
The sun is resplendent against the rain.
The rain is refreshing against the sun.
Grasping the long-term rhythm of the seasons,
Their testiness and cumulative grace,
The mountains maintain their majesty
And proclaim their mastery over calamity.

*5 July 1978*

Kung panay ulan at bagyo lamang
Magiging burak ang mga bundok.
Kung panay araw at tagtuyot lamang
Magiging gabok ang mga bundok.
Ang araw ay marilag laban sa ulan.
Ang ulan ay mapanariwa laban sa araw.
Sa pagsapol sa matagalang ritmo ng mga panahon,
Sa kasungitan at naiipong pagpapala,
Pinamamalagi ng mga bundok ang kanilang katayugan
At ipinapahayag ang pagwawagi sa kalamidad.

*5 Hulyo 1978*

## The North Star Is Always There

Whatever the part of the day,
Whatever the part of the year
The North Star is always there.

No matter how dark the night,
We can trust the light
Of the North Star, our guide.

No matter how thick the clouds,
These are froth ephemeral
The North Star scatters and floats.

Wherever we are, in the woods,
On the plains or at sea,
By the North Star, we see the route.

In the archipelago, come what may,
We have our sure compass,
The North Star is always there.

*March 1979*

## Laging Naroon ang Hilagang Tala

Anuman ang bahagi ng araw,
Anuman ang bahagi ng taon
Laging naroon ang Hilagang Tala.

Gaano man kadilim ang gabi,
Ating maasahan ang liwanag
Ng Hilagang Tala, ating patnubay.

Gaano man kakapal ang mga ulap,
Panandaliang bula ang mga ito
Winawatak at pinalulutang ng Hilagang Tala.

Nasaan man tayo, sa gubat,
Sa kapatagan o sa dagat,
Sa Hilagang Tala, nakikita natin ang ruta.

Sa kapuluan, anuman ang mangyari,
Mayroon tayong tiyak na bruhula,
Laging naroon ang Hilagang Tala.

*Marso 1979*

## In Praise of Martyrs

We praise to high heavens
And for all time
The heroes who die
In the hands of the enemy
In the battlefield
In the torture chamber
And against the wall.
In these bloody places,
The struggle is sharpest
And the meaning of one's life
Is tested in one crucial moment.
Courage to the last breath
Makes the martyr live beyond death.

*9 December 1977*

Papuri sa mga Martir

Abot langit at walang hanggan
Ang papuri natin
Sa mga bayaning namatay
Sa kamay ng kaaway:
Sa larangan ng labanan
Sa silid ng pahirapan
At sa pinaghanayang pader.
Sa madudugong lugar na ito,
Ang pakikibaka'y pinakamatalas
At ang kahulugan ng buhay
Ay nasusubok sa isang mapagpasyang sandali.
Kagitingan hanggang huling hinga
Ang bumubuhay sa martir
Lagpas sa iglap ng kamatayan.

*9 Disyembre 1977*

## Wisdom from a Comrade

A Red fighter had died in the battle
And his sweetheart was grieving.
A comrade went over to her and said,
"He was my best pal and I am also sad
But I am happy too and proud of him
For he was to the end a revolutionary
And nothing can ever change that."
She wiped off her tears and smiled.
When I heard those words and saw her eyes,
I felt the wisdom flow into my soul.

*14 December 1977*

Dunong Mula sa isang Kasama

Isang Pulang mandirigma ang nasawi sa labanan
At nagdalamhati ang kanyang kasintahan.
Isang kasama ang lumapit sa kanya at nagsabi,
"Siya'y pinakamatalik kong katoto't malungkot din ako,
Ngunit masaya rin ako't maipagmamalaki ko siya
Pagkat rebolusyonaryo siya hanggang wakas
At wala kailanman ang makapagbabago nito."
Pinunas niya ang kanyang mga luha at ngumiti.
Nang marinig ko ang sabing iyo't mata niya'y makita,
Dama kong dumaloy ang dunong sa aking kaluluwa.

*14 Disyembre 1977*

What Makes a Hero

It is not the manner of death
That makes a hero.
It is the meaning of life drawn
From the struggles against the foe.

There is the hero who dies in the battlefield,
There is the hero who dies of hunger and disease,
There is the hero who dies of some accident,
There is the hero who dies of old age.

Whatever is the manner of death,
There is the common denominator:
A hero serves the people
To his very last breath.

*10 December 1977*

## Ang Pagiging Bayani

Hindi sa paraan ng kamatayan
Ang pagiging bayani.
Ito'y kahulugang hinango
Sa mga pakikibaka sa kaaway.

May bayaning namamatay sa larangan ng labanan,
May bayaning namamatay sa gutom at sakit,
May bayaning namamatay sa isang aksidente,
May bayaning namamatay sa katandaan.

Anuman ang paraan ng kamatayan,
May pamantayan para sa lahat:
Ang bayani ay naglilingkod sa bayan
Hanggang sa pinakahuli niyang hininga.

*10 Disyembre 1977*

*second part · detention and defiance*

*ikalawang bahagi · pagkapiit at paglaban*

Fragments of a Nightmare

1.
Under the night sky, fresh breaths
Of green leaves and blue waves
Rush to my face, cling to my body
And spur me on to meet my beloved.
As on a hundred steeds, I speed
Like a free bird on a silver ribbon
Between the mountain and the sea.
But alas the unholy hour is fraught
With the dagger eyes of demons
At the junction of haven and danger.

2.
After a monkey dance in the dark
Around the silent transit station,
The demons burst through the flimsy door,
Raise the din of blood lust
And sicken the sudden light.
I am surrounded by armed demons
Prancing and manacling me.
I am wrenched from my beloved
And carried on frenzied wheels
Through the strange cold night.

## Mga Piraso ng Bangungot

1.
Sa ilalim ng langit ng gabi, mga sariwang samyo
Ng mga luntiang dahon at bughaw na alon
Ang sumasalubong sa mukha ko, kumakapit sa katawan ko
At umuudyok na tagpuin ko ang aking mahal.
Wari'y hatak ng sandaang kabayo, humahagibis ako
Tulad ng malayang ibon sa lasong pilak
Sa pagitan ng bundok at dagat.
Ngunit, ay! tigib ang alanganing oras
Ng mga punyal na mata ng mga demonyo
Sa sangandaan ng kaligtasan at panganib.

2.
Matapos ang sayaw-matsing sa dilim
Sa paligid ng tahimik na panandaliang himpilan
Biglang tumagos sa marupok na pinto ang mga demonyo
Nagsisihiyaw ng kahayukang dugo
At ipinanilaw ang biglang liwanag.
Pinaligiran ako ng mga armadong demonyong
Naglulundagan at ako'y pinosasan.
Hinablot ako sa piling ng aking mahal
At isinakay sa tarantang mga gulong
Sa nakakailang na gabing maginaw.

3.
I am brought to the center of hell
To the Devil and his high demons
For a ritual of flashbulbs.
The Devil waves away his minions
And we engage in a duel of words.
For a start, he talks of buying souls.
Repulsed, he shifts to setting
A trap for fools and the innocent.
Repulsed again, he ends with a threat
That he will never see me again.


4.
As if midnight, the tight manacles
And the demons were not enough,
I am blindfolded and moved in circles
A series of boxes swallow me:
A sprawling fort, a certain compound
With a creaking-croaking gate
And finally a cell of utter silence
To which I am roughly plunged.
The demons want me to feel
Blind, lost, suffocating, helpless.


5.
I remove the blindfold and find
Myself in a musty tomb.
I abhor the absence of windows,
The sickly green and muteness

3.
Dinala ako sa sentro ng impyerno
Sa Diyablo at matataas niyang demonyo
Para sa ritwal ng mga bombilyang nagkikislapan.
Suminyas ang Diyablo para umalis kanyang mga alipures
At kami'y nagdwelo sa salita.
Sa simula, sabi niyang namimili siya ng mga kaluluwa.
Nang tinanggihan, bumaling siya sa paglalatag
Ng patibong para sa tanga o walang malay.
Muling tinanggihan, nagwakas siyang may banta
Na ako'y hindi na niya muling makikita.

4.
Ang hatinggabi, ang mahigpit na posas
At ang mga demonyo'y waring di pa sapat.
Ako'y piniringa't pinaikut-ikot.
Sunud-sunod na kahon ang lumamon sa akin:
Isang malawak na kuta, isang tiyak na looban
Na may tarangkahang lumalangingit at kumokokak
At huli'y sa isang selda ng lubos na katahimikan
Ako'y isinadlak nang marahas.
Hangad ng mga demonyong ipadama
Na ako'y bulag, ligaw, sikil, walang laban.

5.
Inalis ko ang piring sa mata at natagpuan
Ang sarili sa inaamag na nitso.
Suklam ako sa kawalan ng bintana,
Sa maputlang luntian at kapipihan

Of the walls and the ceiling,
The deep brown of the shut door,
The dizzying flicker of the dim lamp
And sparse air from an obscure vent.
The pit of my stomach keep turning
And my lungs become congested.

6.
Nameless demons come in relay
To feign cordiality or menace me
And explore my brain and nerves.
I draw circles around them
To gain time for my comrades
And warn them with my disappearance.
I demand my right to counsel,
My right against self-damnation,
The whereabouts of my beloved
And the friends abducted with us.

7.
I am forcibly shorn of my shirt
And it is wound around my face.
One more piece of cloth is tightened
Across my covered eyes and nape.
My hands are cuffed behind my back
So tightly as to numb them.
I am fixed on a wooden chair
And made to wait for my fate

Ng mga dinding at ng kisame,
Sa matinding kayumanggi ng pinid na pinto
Sa nakahihilong kisap-kisap ng malabong bombilya
At sa maramot na pasok ng hangin sa tagong butas.
Bumabaligtad ang aking sikmura
At naninikip ang aking mga baga.

6.
Relyebo ang mga demonyong walang pangalan
Para umastang mapagkaibigan o mapagbanta
At galugarin ang aking utak at damdamin
Pinaikut-ikot ko sila sa usapan
Para magkapanahon ang mga kasama
At mabigyang-babala sa aking pagkawala.
Iginigiit ko ang karapatang magka-abugado,
Ang karapatang huwag ipagkanulo ang sarili,
Alamin ang kinaroroonan ng aking mahal
At mga kaibigang kasama naming dinukot.

7.
Sapilitang inalis ang aking kamisadentro
At ipinulupot ito sa aking mukha.
Isa pang piraso ng damit ang ipinanghigpit
Sa aking nakapiring na mga mata at batok.
Pinosasan sa likod ang aking mga kamay
Nang napakahigpit hanggang sa mamanhid.
Isinalpak ako sa isang silyang kahoy
At pinapaghintay ng aking kapalaran

In utter blindness and helplessness
In the hands of some monster.

8.
All of a sudden sharp fist blows
Strike my floating ribs,
Chest and solar plexus.
Then the demons make barrages
Of questions, threats and taunts
With more barrages of hard blows.
My silence, answer or comment
Always fetches harder blows.
The demons keep on threatening
To break my skull against the wall

9.
The seemingly endless bout ends
But something more is afoot.
The demons chain one of my feet
And one of my hands to a cot.
I remove the blindfolds and my eyes
Are struck by a beam of light
That follows the motion of my face
My eyes outracing the light scan
The dark emptiness of the cell
And make out three demons.

Sa ganap na pagkabulag at kawalan ng magawa
Sa mga kamay ng ilang halimaw.

8.
Biglang dumagsa ang matitinding suntok
Sa lutang kong mga tadyang,
Sa dibdib at sikmura.
Sunod, dagsa-dagsang
Mga tanong, banta at tuya
Sabay dagsa-dagsa pang malakas na suntok.
Ang aking pagtahimik, tugon o puna
Ay laging nagbubunga ng mas matitinding suntok.
Paulit-ulit na nagbabanta ang mga demonyo
Na babasagin ang aking bungo sa pader.

9.
Nagwakas ang wari walang katapusang gulpihan
Subalit mayroon pang namimintong kasunod.
Ikinadena ng mga demonyo ang isang paa ko
At isang kamay ko sa teheras.
Inalis ko ang piring at aking mga mata'y
Pinatamaan ng sinag ng liwanag
Na isinusunod sa galaw ng aking mukha.
Nauunahan ng mga mata ko ang liwanag, tanaw ko
Ang madilim na kahungkagan ng selda
At naaninag ko ang tatlong demonyo.

10.
Two alternate in pointing a gun
At my prostrate body and repeating
Questions I do not care to answer,
While the third sits silent
On the floor of the dark cell.
And one more demon comes and goes
Asking questions and threatening
To kill me in the act of "escaping".
Now and then, a demon kicks
A foot of the cot in exasperation.

11.
In contempt of their menacing form,
I keep telling the demons to take a rest,
Ridicule their words and antics
And hurl back their insults at them
Even as they weaken my body
By keeping me awake, hungry and thirsty.
I can sense being prepared
For a more painful, a worse ordeal.
But I reckon the Devil's order
Is to cause fright and uncertainty.

12.
Once more I am blindfolded
As more demons suddenly swarm
Into the dark stifling cell.
Both my hands and both my feet

10.
Halinhinan ang dalawa sa pagtutok ng baril
Sa lugmok kong katawan at inuulit-ulit
Mga tanong na di ko naman sinasagot
Samantalang ang ikatlo'y tahimik na nakaupo
Sa sahig ng madilim na selda.
At isa pang demonyo ang labas-masok
Para magtanong at magbantang
Ako'y papatayin habang "tumatakas".
Paminsan-minsan, tinatadyakan ng isang demonyo
Ang isang paa ng teheras sa pagkainis.

11.
Sa paghamak sa mapagbantang asta nila,
Maulit kong sinasabi sa mga demonyo na magpahinga,
Tinuya ko ang kanilang mga salita't saltik
At inihagis kong pabalik ang mga insulto nila
Kahit na pinapanghina nila ang aking katawan
Sa patuloy na puyat, gutom at uhaw.
Hinuha kong ako'y inihahanda
Sa mas masakit, mas masahol na pahirap.
Subalit tantya ko ang utos ng Dyablo
Ay manakot at manlito.

12.
Muli akong piniringan
Nang biglang dumagsa ang marami pang demonyo
Sa madilim, nakasisikil na selda.
Dalawang kamay at dalawang paa ko

Are tightly shackled to the cot
With sharp-edged cuffs that tighten
Whenever I make the slightest move.
I hear a demon say my grave is ready
And another say that I should first
Be given electric shocks.

13.
Thoughts race through my mind:
I have met and measured the Devil;
He wants my soul more than my corpse.
These tormentors blindfold me
To conceal their craven faces.
I will suffer but I will endure.
The nerves grow numb against pain;
The brain shuts off against the extreme.
But so what if I die, my life
Has long been given to the cause.

14.
I hear water gushing against water,
The racket of plastic pails
And the screeches of frantic boots.
A small towel is put across my face
And mouth; and strong hands hold
My head and grasp my mouth.
Cascades of water dig into my nostrils
And flood my mouth, throat and lungs.

Mahigpit na ikinadena sa teheras
Gamit ang mga posas na matalim ang gilid at humihigpit
Tuwing galaw ko, kahit pinakabahagya.
Dinig kong sabi ng isang demonyo na hukay ko'y handa na a
At may isa namang nagsabi
Na ako'y dapat kuryentihin muna.

13.
Naghahabulan ang mga isipin sa aking utak.
Nakaharap at nasukat ko ang Dyablo;
Hangad niya ang aking kaluluwa kaysa aking bangkay.
Piniringan ako ng mga tagapagpahirap
Para ikubli ang mga mukha nilang duwag.
Maghihirap ako subalit ako'y mananaig.
Nagiging manhid ang nerbyos laban sa sakit;
Nagpipinid ang utak laban sa sukdulan.
Pero walang anuman kung ako'y mamatay, aking buhay
Matagal nang inilaan sa layon ng pakikibaka.

14.
Dinig ko ang lagaslas ng tubig sa tubig,
Ang kalampag ng mga timbang plastik
At kaluskos ng natatarantang mga botas.
Isang bimpo ang itinapal sa aking mukha
At mata at malalakas na kamay ang humawak
Sa aking ulo at dumaklot sa aking bunganga.
Mga buhos ng tubig ang dumudukal sa aking ilong
At bumabaha sa aking bunganga, lalamunan at baga.

The torrents of water come with torrents
Of questions, threats and taunts.

15.
The cuffs slash my wrists and ankles
As I strain for air again and again
Against the stinging rush of water.
I suffer for so many persons, groups,
Addresses, villages, mountains
That I do not know or do not want
To tell or confirm to the demons.
They are most vicious or persistent
In trying to extract hot leads,
More prey and more spoils.

16.
For more than a thousand times,
The strength of my heart is tested.
As I struggle and scream for air.
American rock music screens my screams
Outside the torture chamber.
From time to time, a demon pokes
The barrel of a gun into my mouth;
Another keeps on jabbing his fingers
Into different parts of my body
To disrupt the rhythm of my resistance.

Kasabay ng dagsa ng tubig ang dagsa
Ng mga tanong, banta at kutya.

15.
Linalaslas ng posas ang galang-galang at bukung-bukong
Sa paulit-ulit kong pagsinghap ng hangin
Laban sa mahapding dagsa ng tubig.
Nagdurusa ako para sa kayraming tao, pangkat,
Tirahan, nayon, bundok
Na hindi ko alam o kaya'y ayaw kong
Sabihin o ikumpirma sa mga demonyo.
Sila'y pinakamalupit at mapagpumilit
Sa pagsubok nilang makapiga ng himatong,
Dagdag na sila at dagdag na dambong.

16.
Higit sa sanlibong ulit
Sinubok ang tibay ng aking puso.
Sa pagpipiglas ko't paghiyaw na makahinga
Mga sigaw ko'y tinatakpan ng tugtuging American rock
Sa labas ng silid ng pahirapan.
Manaka-naka, isinusubo ng isang demonyo
Ang nguso ng baril sa aking bunganga;
Isinusundot ng isa pa ang kanyang mga daliri
Sa iba't ibang bahagi ng aking katawan
Para guluhin ang ritmo ng aking paglaban.

**17.**
My struggles loosen the blindfold.
I can see a senior demon gloating.
Then a stocky demon sits on my belly.
As my body weakens and I grow dizzy,
The chief interrogator vainly tries
To hypnotize me by repeating words,
Suggesting that I am going, going
To sleep and rest my mind in his power.
I resist and keep my wits alive
By recalling the words of a battle cry.

**18.**
The demons fail to drown my spirit
But I am tired and dazed for days.
I lie half-naked shackled to the cot
With wounded wrists and ankles,
Numb hands, chest pains
And pricking sensations in my eyes.
Still I am blindfolded again and again
As vulture demons come in relay
To drum questions into my ears
As if their persistence were endless.

**19.**
I keep on thinking of seagulls
Frail and magical above the blue ocean;
And doves in pairs so gentle,
One partner so close to the other.

17.
Pinaluwag ng aking paglaban ang piring.
Kita kong baliw sa tuwa ang isang mataas na demonyo.
Maya-maya, matabang demonyo ang umupo sa tiyan ko.
Habang nanghihina ang katawan ko't ako'y nahihilo
Bigong tinangka ng pinunong interogador
Na ipailalim ako sa hipnosis sa pag-uulit-ulit ng mga salita,
Na ako'y nahuhulog, nahuhulog sa tulog
At ako'y nagpapaubaya ng isip sa kanyang kapangyarihan.
Ako'y lumalaban at ibayong buhay ang aking isip
Sa pag-alaala ng mga katagang sigaw sa labanan.

18.
Bigong lunurin ng mga demonyo ang aking diwa
Subalit ako'y pagod at hilo nang ilang araw.
Halos hubad akong nakakadena sa teheras
Sugatan ang mga galang-galang at bukung-bukong
Manhid ang mga kamay, may kirot sa dibdib
At parang tinutusok ng karayom ang aking mga mata.
Kahit gayon, paulit-ulit akong pinipiringan
Sa halinhinang pagdating ng mga bwitreng demonyo
Para magtambol ng mga tanong sa aking tainga
Waring walang katapusan ang pagpupumilit nila.

19.
Lagi kong iniisip ang mga kanaway
Maselan at mahiwaga sa itaas ng bughaw na dagat
At ang mga pares na kalapating napakayumi,
Bawat isa'y kay talik sa kanyang katuwang.

I am blindfolded and a vulture demon
Comes to insult me with an offer:
To be caged with my beloved
In return for one free comrade.
I grit my teeth and grunt at the demon
And wish that I could do more to his face.

20.
I see the smiling faces of demons
Who come to make another offer:
I simply declare formally
That I am A. G. and nothing more;
And the torture would cease
And I would be placed where
Other captives of the Devil are.
They even agree to an indication
That access to counsel is impossible
Because of the armed demons themselves.

21
The torture does not cease
But becomes worse a thousand times.
The seconds, minutes, days, weeks,
Months and seasons fall
Like huge blocks of lead
On my brain and nerves,
On my prostrate body on the rack,
With my left hand and right foot

Piniringan ako at isang bwitreng demonyo
Ang dumating para insultuhin ako ng isang alok::
Makulong kapiling ang aking mahal
Kapalit ng isang kasamang nasa laya.
Nagngitngit ako't umungol sa demonyo
At ninais kong sapukin ang kanyang mukha.

20.
Kita ko ang mga nakangisngis na demonyo
Na dumating na may isa pang alok :
Simpleng ipahayag ko nang pormal
Na ako si A. G., at walang iba pa;
At matitigil ang pagpapahirap
At ako ay ilalagay sa piitan
Ng iba pang bihag ng Dyablo.
Sumang-ayon pa sila sa isang hiwatig
Na imposible ang pag-ugnay sa abugado
Dahil sa mga armadong demonyo mismo.

21
Walang lubay ang pagpapahirap
Kundi sanlibong ulit na lalo pang lumalala.
Ang mga segundo, minuto, araw, linggo,
Buwan at panahon ay bumabagsak
Na parang malalaking bloke ng tingga
Sa aking utak at nerbyos
Sa handusay kong katawan sa pahirapan,
Ang kaliwang kamay at kanang paa

Constantly cuffed to a filthy cot
In a perpetuated process of violence.

22.
Thick calluses grow where the irons
Press against my flesh and bones.
And I suffer the extremes
Of heat and cold upon the change
Of seasons and the part of a day.
I see nothing beyond the dusty walls
And cobwebbed ceiling.
Day and night, every ten minutes,
A demon peeps through a small hole
To make sure I remain in shackles.

23.
Only bedbugs, mosquitoes, ants,
Cockroaches, lizards and spiders
Are my cohabitants in this part of hell
I miss and yearn for my beloved
And think of her own fate.
I long for my growing children;
I long for the honest company
Of workers, peasants and comrades.
I long for the people rising
And the wide open spaces of my country.

Laging nakakadena sa maruming teheras
Sa pinamalaging pandarahas.

22.
Makakapal na kalyo ang tumubo
Sa dinidiinan ng bakal sa laman at buto ko.
At naghihirap ako sa kalabisan
Ng init at lamig sa pagbabago
Ng panahon o bahagi ng isang araw.
Wala akong nakikitang lampas sa magabok na dinding
At masapot na kisame.
Araw at gabi, bawat sampung minuto
Sumisilip sa maliit na butas ang isang demonyo
Para tiyaking laging nakakadena ako.

23.
Tanging mga surot, lamok, langgam
Ipis, butiki at gagamba
Ang kasama ko sa bahaging ito ng impyerno.
Hinahanap at pinanabikan ko ang aking mahal
At iniisip ko ang sarili niyang kinasapitan.
Sabik ako sa lumalaki kong mga anak
Sabik ako sa matapat na samahan
Ng mga manggagawa, magbubukid at kasama
Sabik ako sa mga mamamayang nagsisialsa
At sa malapad at bukas na kalawakan ng aking bayan.

24.
The imps who detach me from the cot
Are tightlipped most of the time
And show insolence, harass and insult me
Whenever they think I am going beyond
The few minutes allowed me to eat
Bad food and perform necessities.
The demon doctor merely smiles
When I ask for fresh air and sunlight.
The demon dentist does not repair
But keep on busting my teeth.

25.
Some demons come now and then
Asking why I wish to suffer
When all I need is to surrender
My soul for the Devil's compassion.
Asked once to run for an assembly
Of demons, I retort how can I run
When I cannot even walk in my cell.
Then, even they stop coming,
To let me suffer without respite
The flames of one summer after another.

26.
As I refuse to sell or give away
My soul to the Devil, his scheme
Is to torment and kill it slowly
By fixing my body on the rack,

**24**
Ang mga impaktong nagkakalag sa akin
Ay karaniwang tikom ang mga bibig
At pakita'y kawalang galang, nanggigipit at nang-iinsulto
Kailanma't iniisip nilang lumalagpas ako
Sa ilang minutong laan para kumain
Ng panis at magbanyo't kubeta.
Ngumingisi lamang ang demonyong doktor
Kapag humihiling ako ng sariwang hangin at sinag ng araw.
Hindi inaayos ng demonsyong dentista,
Manapa'y sinisira pa ang aking ngipin.

**25**
Ilang demonyo'y dumarating paminsan-minsan
Nagtatanong bakit nais kong maghirap
Gayong tanging dapat kong gawin ay isuko
Ang aking kaluluwa sa habag ng Diyablo.
Minsan akong hiniling na tumakbo para sa asambleya
Ng mga demonyo, pakli ko'y paano ako tatakbo
Gayong di man ako makalakad sa selda ko.
Pagkatapos, maging sila'y tumigil sa pagdating
Upang paghirapin ako nang walang tigil
Sa liyab ng sunud-sunod na tag-init.

**26.**
Habang tumatanggi akong ipagbili o ipamigay
Ang kaluluwa ko sa Dyablo, pakana niya
Ang pahirapan at patayin ito nang dahan-dahan
Sa paggapos ng aking katawan sa pahirapan,

Dangling the sword of death
And threatening to let it fall
By some formal or informal process.
But the scheme is futile
As the agony of isolation in shackles
Even makes death a tempting recourse.

27.
I struggle against the tedium,
The cumulative stress on my body and mind
And occasional lure of suicide.
I keep on composing and reciting poems
To damn the Devil and the demons.
I keep on summoning images
Of my beloved suffering but enduring;
Our free and fast-growing children;
And the masses of avenging angels
Armed with the sharpest of swords.

28.
Every day that passes is a day won,
Heightening will and endurance.
I anticipate the Devil's pretense–
Bringing me to his court for a show
And having the demon judges acclaim him
As supreme lawmaker, captor, torturer,
Prosecutor, judge and executioner.
After so long in the rack, I can sit

Amba ng espada ng kamatayan
At bantang ipatihulog ito
Sa paraang pormal o impormal.
Subalit pakana'y walang saysay
Habang ang pighati ng solitaryong pagkakadena
Ay nanunuksong dulugan kahit kamatayan.

27.
Binabaka ko ang pagkabagot,
Ang pag-ipon ng igting sa aking katawan at isip
At ang pasumpong na halina na kitilin ang sarili.
Patuloy akong kumakatha at bumibigkas ng tula
Para sumpain ang Dyablo at mga demonyo.
Lagi kong ginugunita ang mga larawan
Ng aking mahal, nagdurusa subalit nananaig;
Ng aming mga anak na malaya't mabilis lumaki;
Ng masa ng naghihiganting mga anghel
Armado ng pinakamatalas na espada.

28.
Bawat araw na lumipas ay araw na napagtagumpayan,
Nagpapataas ng kapasyahan at katatagan.
Inaabangan ko ang pagkukunwari ng Dyablo:
Ihaharap ako sa hukuman niyang palabas
At ipagbubunyi siya ng mga demonyong huwes
Bilang kataas-taasang mambabatas, tagahuli, tagapagpahirap
Tagausig, huwes at berdugo.
Matapos ang kaytagal sa pahirapan, makakaupo ako

Beside my beloved before the demon judges
And let the people know our ordeal.

29.
To speak of torture in hindsight,
To speak of one-hour punching,
So many meals and hours of sleep lost,
Six hours of suffocation by water,
Eighteen months on the rack
And so many years of cramped seclusion,
Is never to say enough of suffering.
The Devil and the demons never tell
The victim when a certain ordeal ends
Even as they threaten more pain and death.

30.
But still my pain and suffering is small
As I think of those who suffer more
The violence of daily exploitation
And the rampage of terror on the land.
I belittle my pain and suffering
As I think of the people who fight
For their own redemption and freedom
And avenge the blood of martyrs.
I belittle my pain and suffering
As I hope to give more to the struggle.

*December 1979*

Sa tabi ng aking mahal sa harap ng mga demonyong huwes
At ipababatid sa mamamayan ang dinanas naming pahirap.

29.
Ang magsalita tungkol sa pahirap pagkapangyari ng lahat
Ang magsalita tungkol sa isang oras na pambubugbog,
Kayraming ipinagkait na pagkain at oras ng pagtulog,
Anim na oras ng panlulunod sa tubig
Labingwalong buwan ng pagkakagapos
At kayraming taon ng sikil na pag-iisa,
Ay di kailanman sasapat sa paliwanag ng pagdurusa.
Ang Dyablo at mga demonyo ay di kailanman magsasabi
Sa biktima kung kailan matatapos ang pahirap
Habang nagbabanta sila ng ibayong sakit at kamatayan.

30.
Gayunpama'y maliit ang aking hirap at dusa
Habang iniisip ko yaong higit na naghihirap
Sa dahas ng araw-araw na pagsasamantala
At pagragasa ng lagim sa bayan.
Minamaliit ko ang aking hirap at dusa
Habang iniisip ko ang mamamayang lumalaban
Para sa kanilang katubusan at kalayaan
At ipinaghihiganti ang dugong ibinuwis ng mga martir.
Mimanaliit ko ang aking hirap at dusa
Habang umaasa akong makaambag pa sa pakikibaka.

*Disyembre 1979*

## In the Dark Depths

The enemy wants to bury us
In the dark depths of prison
But shining gold is mined
From the dark depths of the earth
And the radiant pearl is dived
From the dark depths of the sea.
We suffer but we endure
And draw up gold and pearl
From depths of character
Formed so long in struggle.

*10 April 1978*

## Sa Madilim na Kailaliman

Gusto ng kaaway na tayo'y ibaon
Sa madilim na kailaliman ng piitan
Pero ang gintong maningning ay minimina
Sa madilim na kailaliman ng lupa
At ang makinang na perlas ay sinisisid
Sa madilim na kailaliman ng dagat.
Nagdurusa tayo subalit nagtitiis
At humahango ng ginto at perlas
Mula sa kailaliman ng katangiang
Hinubog nang kaytagal sa pakikibaka.

*10 Abril 1978*

Pearl

In the gloomy depths of the ocean,
Pearl is formed by salted pain
In the tenderness of the oyster
In utter cold, under the weight
Of the water mountain of affliction.

The diver cannot reach the pearl
Without weighing himself down,
Without the endurance and painful labor,
Without the keenness of vision
Through the gloom under pressure.

The pearl is the lustrous fruit
Of the oyster's mighty struggle.
It is also a glowing eyeball,
A witness to the diver's effort.
Snatched from the jaws of fathoms,
It becomes a centerpiece of triumph

*12 April 1978*

Perlas

Sa mapanglaw na pusod ng dagat
Binubuo ang perlas ng inasnang kirot
Sa kalambutan ng talaba
Sa sukdulang lamig, sa ilalim ng bigat
Ng bundok-tubig ng dusa.

Hindi maaabot ng maninisid ang perlas
Nang wala siyang pabigat
Nang walang pagtitiis at mahirap na paggawa,
Nang walang matalas na pananaw
Na tagos sa panglaw sa ilalim ng presyon.

Ang perlas ay makinang na bunga
Ng malakas na pakikibaka ng talaba.
Ito rin ay makinang na mata,
Saksi sa pagsisikap ng maninisid..
Dahil inagaw sa panga ng kailaliman,
Nagiging tampok na hiyas ng tagumpay.

*12 Abril 1978*

# Gold

In the dark bowels of the earth,
Under the mountain of pressure,
That gathers the heat of the sun,
Gold is trapped and imprisoned
But gleams with collected fervor.

The miner cannot reach the ore
Without making a deepgoing shaft,
Without exerting painful labor,
Without a longlasting lamp
Through darkness under pressure.

Fiery furnace and acid bowl
Remove dross and refine gold.
Then the fashioning tools turn
To make the crown of triumph
That is the lofty glory of the nation.

*12 April 1978*

# Ginto

Sa mapanglaw na kailaliman ng lupa
Sa diin ng bundok
Na nag-iipon ng init ng araw
Ang ginto'y nabibitag at nabibihag
Ngunit kumikislap sa natipong alab.

Hindi maaabot ng minero ang ginto
Nang di huhukay ng malalimang tunel
Nang di puspusan ang mahirap na paggawa
Nang walang lamparang nagtatagal
Sa karimlan sa ilalim ng presyon.

Pugong nag-aapoy at mangkok ng asido
Ang nag-aalis sa dumi at nagdadalisay ng ginto
Saka iikot ang mga gamit panghugis
Upang gawin ang korona ng tagumpay
Na siyang matayog na kaluwalhatian ng bansa.

*12 Abril 1978*

Chemistry of Tears

Tears have too long been
the food of the meek.

But hunger has become
anger so fierce,

Turning the tears of the meek
into nitroglycerine

To explode the vile system
of terror and greed.

Such is the chemistry of tears
catalyzed by iniquity.

*14 April 1978*

# Kimika ng Luha

Kaytagal nang mga luha
Ang naging pagkain ng maamo.

Ngunit ang gutom ay naging
Galit na kaybangis,

Ang luha ng maamo
Ay naging nitrogliserina

Para pasabugin ang imbing sistema
Ng lagim at kasakiman.

Ganyan ang kimika ng luhang
Katalisado ng katampalasanan.

*14 Abril 1978*

## A Furnace

When it was December
I compared my cell
By midnight to a freezer
And by midday to an oven.

Now that it is summer
I compare it to hell.
But because of its smallness,
I also call it a furnace.

'Tis a seething furnace
For tempering steel
And purifying gold.
'Tis a comforting metaphor.

*15 March 1978*

## Pugon

Noong Disyembre,
Inihambing ko ang aking selda
Sa priser kapag hatinggabi
At sa hurno naman kapag tanghaling-tapat.

Ngayong tag-init na
Inihahambing ko ito sa impyerno,
Pero dahil sa kaliitan nito
Binansagan ko rin itong pugon.

Ito'y nag-aapoy na pugon
Para pandayin ang bakal
At dalisayin ang ginto.
Nakagiginhawa ang talinghaga.

*15 Marso 1978*

## A Cool Breeze

A cool breeze blows into prison
It refreshes the body and warms the soul.
It caresses, kisses and whispers,
"In prison, there is worthy struggle."

The breeze carries the scent of the red flowers,
It is part of the great irresistible wind
Of struggle sweeping all the islands.
Everywhere the message is to fight and win.

*14 December 1977*

Sariwang Simoy

Isang sariwang simoy ang humihip sa piitan
Pinapanariwa ang katawan at pinasisigla ang diwa.
Nanunuyo, humahalik at bumubulong,
"Sa bilangguan, may mahalagang pakikibaka."

Hatid ng simoy ang halimuyak ng mga pulang bulaklak,
Bahagi ito ng malakihang di-mapigil na hangin
Ng pakikibakang sumasaklaw sa lahat ng isla.
Bawat dako ang paabot ay lumaban at magtagumpay.

*14 Disyembre 1977*

## Like a Giant, Like a Bird

In the concrete conditions of prison,
The devil has a big advantage.
Even the demons press their power,
Swaggering like big monsters.

They call the prisoner an ant
They can fool and play with.
But the revolutionary spirit can win,
Whatever is the devil's scheme.

No matter how tight the cell,
It is an arena of struggle,
A part of the wide front
Of the people's surging resistance.

The courageous fight in prison
Joins the irresistible tide
Of the revolutionary struggle springing
From the bosom of the motherland.

Crush the body of the prisoner
Who has a firm and lofty stand,
His spirit resists and endures.
It lives on in the spirit of the masses.

## Tulad ng Higante, Tulad ng Ibon

Sa kongkretong kalagayan ng bilangguan,
Napakalaki ang lamang ng diyablo.
Pati mga demonyo'y nagdidiin ng kapangyarihan nila
Kumakayangkang tulad ng malalaking halimaw.

Tinatawag nilang langgam ang bilanggo
Na maloloko at mapaglalaruan nila.
Ngunit makakapanaig ang diwang rebolusyonaryo,
Anuman ang pakana ng diyablo.

Gaano man kasikip ang selda,
Isang arena ito ng pakikibaka,
Bahagi ng malawak na larangan
Ng dumadaluyong na pakikibaka ng bayan..

Ang magiting na laban sa bilangguan
Ay dumurugtong sa di-mapigil na agos
Ng rebolusyonaryong pakikibakang bumubukal
Sa dibdib ng inang-bayan.

Durugin man ang katawan ng bilanggong
Matatag at matayog ang paninindigan,
Ang kanyang diwa'y lumalaban at nananatili.
Patuloy na nabubuhay sa diwa ng masa.

The heroic prisoner is like a giant;
He draws strength from the masses,
His spirit is like a bird looking down:
Oh, how small are all the monsters below!

*16 December 1977*

Ang bayaning bilanggo ay tulad ng higante;
Humahango siya ng lakas mula sa masa,
Ang kanyang diwa ay tulad ng ibong tumatanaw:
Ah, kayliit ng lahat ng halimaw sa ibaba!

*16 Disyembre 1977*

## My Poems Are Militant

Since a long, long time ago
Incantations and prayers
Have been a comfort
To those who suffer.

Lying down at night,
I recite my poems
Until my throat runs dry
And fall asleep in comfort.

But my poems are militant.
They appeal to the people.
I put my trust in them
And in their firm struggle.

While at rest I am sure
That the struggle goes on.
And when my rest is over
I will do what I can.

Solitary confinement
Is torture so vicious.
But the poems I compose
Are my ardent companions.

*10 May 1978*

## Militante ang mga Tula Ko

Sa mahabang, mahabang panahon,
Mga ingkantasyon at panalangin
Nagiging pampanatag-loob
Sa mga nagdurusa.

Habang nakahiga sa gabi,
Binibigkas ko ang aking mga tula
Hanggang matuyo ang aking lalamunan
At makatulog nang panatag.

Ngunit militante ang mga tula ko.
Nananawagan sa taumbayan.
May tiwala ako sa kanila
At sa matatag nilang pakikibaka.

Habang nagpapahinga natitiyak ko
Na patuloy ang pakikibaka.
At kapag tapos na ang aking pahinga
Gagawin ko ang makakayanan.

Ang na mag-isapagkakulong
Ay napakabuktot na parusa.
Ngunit ang mga tula kong kinakatha
Ay marubdob kong mga kasama.

*10 Mayo 1978*

## I Am Determined To Rise

The demons are laughing;
They say I have fallen.
But the people's movement
In the whole country is advancing.

The red flag flies high,
Wafted by a powerful wind –
The thought that broadcasts
The seeds of the revolution.

The seeds grow so fast
In the soil made fertile
By the sweat and blood of heroes.
Here victory is certain to be reaped.

It is as if I did not stumble
So long as the cadres and fighters
Continue to arise from the masses.
I am determined to rise.

The devil himself shall weep
Over a kingdom of ash heaps.

*8 December 1977*

## May Pasya Akong Bumangon

Halakhakan ang mga demonyo;
Sabi nila bumagsak na ako.
Ngunit ang kilusang-bayan
Sa buong bansa ay sumusulong.

Mataas ang wagayway ng pulang bandila,
Dala ng makapangyarihang hangin–
Ang kaisipang naghahasik
Ng mga binhi ng rebolusyon.

Kay bilis lumago ng mga binhi
Sa lupang pinataba
Ng pawis at dugo ng mga bayani.
Dito tiyak na aanihin ang tagumpay.

Waring hindi ako nadapa
Basta't ang mga kadre at mandirigma
Patuloy na bumabangon mula sa masa.
May pasya akong bumangon.

Kalauna'y hahagulhol ang diyablo mismo
Sa pagkatupok ng kanyang reyno.

*8 Disyembre 1977*

## My Spiritual Weapon

Marxism is a powerful beacon
To revolutionary mass actions.
But in my prolonged isolation
It is also my spiritual weapon.

Wielding it, I defend my integrity;
The enemy cannot overwhelm me.
He is despicable and puny.
Before the people and history.

I draw strength from the revolution
In steady progress outside prison.
I wish to make a contribution
By my struggle even in isolation.

Thus, I can endure the torture,
The physical and mental pressure
And all the diabolic overtures
That the revolution I abdure.

I keep on recalling the people,
Comrades and red fighters
Who have shed their blood in struggle.
My own suffering I belittle.

## Ang Aking Sandatang Pandiwa

Makapangyarihang parola ang Marxismo
Sa rebolusyonaryong mga kilos masa.
Ngunit sa aking matagal na pag-iisa
Ito rin ang aking sandatang pandiwa.

Tangan ito, dangal ko'y aking ipinagtatanggol;
Hindi ako magagahis ng kaaway
Siya'y kasuklam-suklam at mahina
Sa harap ng bayan at kasaysayan.

Humahango ako ng lakas sa rebolusyong
Matatag na sumusulong sa labas ng piitan.
Hangad kong maiambag
Ang aking pakikibaka kahit ako'y mag-isa.

Kaya, natitiis ko ang labis na pahirap,
Ang panggigipit sa katawa't isip
At lahat ng malasatanas na alok
Na itakwil ko ang rebolusyon.

Lagi kong inaala-ala ang mga mamamayan,
Mga kasama at pulang mandirigmang
Nagtitigis ng dugo sa pakikibaka.
Minamaliit ko ang sarliling paghihirap.

I have undergone only punches,
Water cure and daily threats.
But the most difficult of my tests
Is month after month of forced rest.

To a cot I am always shackled
With nothing to read and no spectacles.
It is taxing to the mind and nonsensical
To stare at the ceiling and walls.

I suffer so many deprivations
That boredom and vexation
Often try to close in on my isolation.
But Marxism is my powerful weapon.

I become my own companion
And apply the law of contradiction
On so many problems and questions
In my situation and contemplations.

My interrogators wish information
But I go into political discussion.
I uphold the justness of the revolution,
The people's demands and aspirations.

Due process and basic necessities
I demand without cease,
To struggle on, Marxism tells me,
Against the viciousness of the enemy.

Ang dinanas ko lamang ay bugbog,
Parusa sa tubig at arawang banta.
Ngunit pinakamahirap na pagsubok sa akin
Ang maraming buwan ng sapilitang pahinga.

Lagi akong nakakadena sa teheras
Nang walang mabasa at walang salamin.
Ito ay nakakarindi sa isip at walang kabuluhan
Ang tumitig sa kisame at mga pader.

Nagdurusa ako sa kay raming pagkakait
Na ikinasisidhi ng yamot at inis
Na malimit na nanggigipit sa isang nakawalay.
Ngunit Marxismo ang makapangyarihang sandata ko.

Nagiging kaulayaw ko ang sarili
At inilalapat ko ang batas ng kontradiksyon
Sa kay daming problema at tanong
Sa aking kalagayan at paglilimi.

Nais ng mga interogador ko ay impormasyon
Ngunit dinadala ko sila sa tagisang pampulitika.
Pinaninindigan ko ang katarungan ng rebolusyon,
Ang mga kailangan at hangad ng bayan.

Ang karampatang proseso, mga batayang kailangan
Ipinaggugumiit kong walang tantan,
Upang magpatuloy na makibaka, sabi sa akin ng Marxismo,
Laban sa kabuktutan ng kaaway.

I turn to composing poetry
Expressing my desire to be free
Blending it to the ever fierce
Desire of the people to be free.

I long for the warmth of the people
And full initiative in the struggle.
But each day longer in the present crucible
Tests and tempers the mettle.

A day that passes is a day closer
To the riddance of my shackles.
I place my hopes on the struggle
Of the broad masses of the people.

*8 February 1978*

Bumaling ako sa pagkatha ng mga tula
Para ihayag ang pagnanasa kong lumaya
Para ilahok ito sa laging matinding
Pagnanais ng bayan na lumaya.

Inaasam ko ang sigla ng mamamayan
At ang ganap na inisyatiba sa pakikibaka.
Ngunit sa bawat araw na ako'y nasa pugon
Nasusubok at napapanday ang aking katatagan.

Isang araw na lumipas ay isang araw na malapit
Sa pagtanggal sa aking mga kadena.
Isinasalalay ko ang aking pag-asa sa pakikibaka
Ng malawak na masa ng sambayanan.

*8 Pebrero 1978*

## Nothing More Beautiful

I decided a long time ago
That if I were imprisoned
I would do as Comrade Ho,
To write revolutionary poems.

The movement was on the rise
When he was put behind bars.
As he sang of the grain of rice
Made pearl white, he never lost touch.

I think of all the reasons
That in due time I shall be out.
I am sure that the passage of seasons
Will further shed from victory any doubt.

Meanwhile, there's nothing more beautiful
Than to sing songs of freedom,
Songs of the people's struggle,
To fight tyranny and boredom.

A spirit as active and free as mine
Can never be entombed in a cell.
I shall continue to rise
In defiance of the somnolent bell.

*30 December 1977*

## Walang Mas Maganda

Matagal na akong nagpasya
Na kung ako'y mabilanggo
Tutularan ko ang ginawa ni Kasamang Ho,
Ang magsulat ng mga tulang rebolusyonaryo.

Papalakas ang kilusan
Nang siya'y ibilanggo.
Habang umaawit ukol sa butil ng bigas
Na naging simbusilak ng perlas, di siya nawalay.

Iniisip ko ang lahat ng dahilan
Na ako'y lalaya sa kalaunan.
Tiyak ko na sa pagdaan ng panahon
Lalaho ang anumang alinlangan sa tagumpay.

Samantala, walang mas maganda
Sa pag-awit ng mga kanta ng paglaya
Mga kanta ng pakikibaka ng mamamayan
Upang labanan ang paniniil at bagot.

Ang diwang kasing aktibo at kasing laya ng sa akin
Ay di kailanman maililibing sa isang selda
Patuloy akong babangon
Laban sa mapanglaw na batingaw.

*30 Disyembre 1977*

## I Am Always with You

My body is in prison
But my spirit freely roams
Every region and zone
In every season.

What I have done
For so long in the revolution
Cannot at one blow be undone.
It is by you carried on.

When I was arrested,
The revolutionary forces
Were far from the scratch
Where they started.

Dare to continue the ascent.
Don't let anyone's stumble
Disrupt our great movement.
Raise the red flag ever higher.

I am always with you,
In your studies, work and battles,
I am always with you,
Carrying out our urgent tasks.

## Lagi Ko Kayong Kasama

Nasa bilangguan ang aking katawan
Ngunit malayang lumilibot ang aking diwa
Sa bawat rehiyon at sona
Sa bawat panahon.

Ang aking ginawa
Nang kay tagal sa rebolusyon
Hindi mapapawi sa isang bigwas.
Kayo ang nagpapatuloy.

Nang ako'y arestuhin,
Ang mga rebolusyonaryong pwersa
Malayo na sa kahig
Na kanilang pinagsimulan.

Mangahas na ipagpatuloy ang pag-akyat.
Huwag hayaan na ang pagkadapa ninuma'y
Ikapatid ng ating dakilang kilusan.
Lalo pang itaas ang pulang bandila .

Lagi ko kayong kasama,
Sa inyong pag-aaral, gawain at laban,
Lagi ko kayong kasama,
Sa pagtupad ng ating mahihigpit na tungkulin.

I share with you
Your weal and woe,
I am always in the line
Of march with you.

Cover the whole country;
Go deep in every locality;
Overcome every difficulty;
Ensure our victory.

*26 December 1977*

Kabahagi ninyo ako
Sa hirap at ginhawa,
Lagi ko kayong kasama
Sa linya ng martsa.

Saklawin ang buong bansa;
Magpalalim sa bawat lokalidad;
Pangibabawan ang bawat kahirapan;
Tiyakin ang ating tagumpay.

*26 Disyembre 1977*

## You Are My Wife and Comrade

You are my wife and comrade.
It is harsh that we are kept apart
By a cruel enemy with many snares.
We care for each other's welfare.

The wishes of the tyrant are so evil.
He seeks the betrayal of our souls
By torture and the threat of murder
And the wasting away of our youthful vigor

His cruel minions are gleeful
That we suffer in stifling cubicles.
They are driven by usurped power
And like dogs carry out orders.

But even in our forced separation
We remain one in fierce devotion
To the noble cause of the revolution.
Firmly the struggle we must carry on.

Our chief tormentor on the throne
Will someday be overthrown.
For the seed has been sown
And the future is well known.

## Asawa Kita at Kasama

Asawa kita at kasama.
Marahas tayong pinaghiwalay
Ng malupit na kaaway na marami ang patibong.
Kumakalinga tayo sa isa't-isa.

Kay buktot ang nasa ng maniniil.
Nais niyang ating ipagkanulo ang mga kaluluwa natin
Sa labis na pahirap at banta ng pagpaslang
At pag-aksaya sa ating bulas na lakas.

Galak ang kanyang malulupit na kampon
Na pagdusahin tayo sa mga mapanakal na silid
Inuudyukan sila ng kamkam na kapangyarihan
At mala-aso nilang tinutupad ang mga utos.

Ngunit kahit sapilitan tayong pinaghiwalay
Magkakaisa pa rin tayo sa marubdob na pagmamahalan
Sa marangal na layon ng rebolusyon.
Matatag nating dapat ipagpatuloy ang pakikibaka.

Ang ating punong tagapagpahirap na nasa trono
Ay ibabagsak balang araw.
Pagkat naipunla na ang binhi
At ang hinaharap ay alam na alam na.

We have lived a full and fruitful life
Even at a youthful age so rife
For so much more to be done
In the raging course of the revolution.

We fear neither hardship nor death
For the people's supreme interest.
We are scornful of slander and intrigue
As the people wait for us to speak.

We may never be allowed to speak.
But tongues of fire affirm our integrity.
More than enough are the testaments
For our children's worthy heritage.

We miss our beloved children
But our spirit continues to guide them.
We will always be part of the movement
Far beyond the bounds of the present.

*10 March 1978*

Puno at mabunga na ang ating buhay
Kahit na sa batang gulang na lipos
Ng kay rami pang gagawin
Sa rumaragasang takbo ng rebolusyon.

Wala tayong takot sa hirap o kamatayan
Sa kataas-taasang kapakanan ng bayan.
Itinatanggi natin ang paninirang-puri at intriga
Habang naghihintay ang bayan na tayo'y magsalita.

Maaaring hindi na tayo pagsalitain kailanman,
Ngunit patunay ang mga dila ng apoy sa ating katapatan
Higit na sa sapat ang mga kasulatan
Na makabuluhang pamana natin sa mga anak.

Nangungulila tayo sa mga anak nating minamahal
Ngunit ang diwa nati'y patuloy na pumapatnubay sa kanila.
Lagi tayong bahagi ng kilusan
Malayong lampas sa mga hanggahan ng kasalukuyan.

*10 Marso 1978*

Across Blue Waters

*To Janah, János & Jemmima*

In a flash, so many years
Of separation slyly flee,
Chased by ceaseless tasks
Of Mama's, mine and yours.

Across blue waters
We smile to each other.
For us to embrace and kiss
We dispatch the waves.

We feel the strong currents
Move from shore to shore
Like cords binding us,
Exhorting the warmth of love.

Our love rides the waves
And, lofted to the air,
Takes wings and sings
In the gleeful winds.

What is a spray of salt
That we sometimes taste

Sa Ibayong Dagat na Asul

*Kina Janah, János & Jemmima*

Sa isang iglap, kay raming taon
Ng pagkahiwalay ang kubling tumakas
Hinahabol ng walang humpay na mga tungkulin
Ng inyong Ina, akin at ninyo.

Sa ibayong dagat na asul
Nagngingitian tayo sa isa't isa.
Para magyakapan at maghalikan,
Sinusugo natin ang mga alon.

Dama natin ang malalakas na agos
Mula sa dalampasigan tungo sa kabila
Tulad ng mga taling nagbibigkis sa atin,
Nagpapaalab sa ating pagmamahalan.

Sumasakay ang ating pag-ibig sa mga alon
At, sa pagkakahagis sa himpapawid.
Ay nagkakapakpak at umaawit
Sa masayahing hangin.

Ano man lang ang wisik ng asin
Na minsan-minsa'y natitikman natin

As we in laughter embrace
The ever surging waves?

We scorn time and space
As measures of our distance
For we seize both on each shore
in shared cause and hopes.

The sea does not divide us
But links our mutual lives
Under the red star or sun
That on both shores shine.

In sharing thoughts and joys
And conquering whatever pains,
We strengthen our oneness
As if we have never parted.

*6 December 1981*

Habang nagtatawanang yakap natin
Ang mga along laging sumusulong?

Hinahamak natin ang panahon at kalawakan
Bilang mga panukat ng ating pagitan
Dahil inaagaw natin ang dalawa sa bawat baybayin
Sa pinagkaisahang layunin at mga pangarap.

Hindi tayo hinahati ng dagat
Kundi pinagdurugtong nito ang kapwa nating buhay
Sa sinag ng pulang bituin o araw
Na tumatanglaw sa ating mga dalampasigan.

Sa bahaginan ng isipan at ligaya
At sa pananaig sa anumang sakit,
Pinalalakas natin ang pagkakaisa
Na wari di tayo naghiwalay kailanman.

*6 Disyembre 1981*

## To Jasm, My Captive Child

Radiance on the face of mother,
Where the sun is banned,
You were already a prisoner
Beyond the warmth of the womb.

You have freed yourself
From one enclosure to another,
To a blind tomb built by ogres
Who shun the birth of a new life.

So soon are you robbed
Of green earth, streams, fresh wind,
Raging flowers and chirping birds,
Sun, moon and stars in the sky.

What have you in this shut-in space?
Sickening heat most of the day,
The intrusion of dust and gas fumes
And sudden cold in the night.

You are the child of captives
And you must share their life
As the compassion of tyranny
Finds every reason for cruelty.

## Kay Jasm, Anak Ko sa Piitan

Ningning sa mukha ng ina
Kung saan ipinagkait ng araw,
Ika'y naging bilanggo na
Paglabas sa init ng sinapupunan.

Pinalaya mo ang sarili
Mula sa isang kulungan tungo sa isa pa,
Isang bulag na nitsong itinayo ng mga halimaw
Na suklam sa pagsilang ng bagong buhay.

Kay agang ninakawan ka
Ng luntiang lupa, batis, sariwang hangin,
Makukulay na bulaklak at ibong nagsisiawit,
Araw, buwan at mga bituin sa langit.

Ano ang sa iyo sa kulungang ito?
Nakakaduwal na init halos buong araw,
Panghihimasok ng alikabok at sansang ng gasolina
At biglaang ginaw sa gabi.

Anak ka ng mga bilanggo
At sapilitang kasama ka sa buhay nila
Habang ang habag ng maniniil
Ay laging may dahilang magmalupit

And yet our joy is boundless.
We crowd this room with our love,
Defy the arrogant walls
And reach out to those who care.

Were you freed from this cell,
There is still a larger prison
Where the people must struggle
To win the sphere of freedom.

Life is a series of struggles
Against definite kinds of prison.
As you grow, you will know freedom
Is won as at your birthing.

Someday you will be proud
That since birth you have been
In the thick of struggle.
Thus, we call you our Jasm.

Feed well from the breast
Of your mother the courage
And strength to bring down
The walls of tyranny in the land.

*January 1982*

Gayunman, ang ating ligaya ay walang hangganan.
Pinupuno natin ang silid na ito ng ating pag-iibigan,
Labanan ang mga palalong pader
At magpaabot tayo sa mga may malasakit.

Paglaya mo sa seldang ito,
Mayroon pang mas malaking bilangguan
Kung saan dapat makibaka ang bayan
Upang ipanalo ang saklaw ng kalayaan.

Ang buhay ay sunud-sunod na pakikibaka
Laban sa iba't ibang klase ng bilangguan.
Sa paglaki mo, iyong malalaman na ang laya
Ipinapanalo tulad ng iyong pagsilang.

Balang araw maipagmamalaki mo
Na mula noong ipinanganak ka
Nasa gitna ka na ng pakikibaka.
Kaya tinatawag ka naming aming Jasm.

Susuhin mong mabuti mula sa dibdib
Ng iyong ina ang giting
At lakas upang ibagsak
Ang mga pader ng paniniil sa bayan.

*Enero 1982*

*third part · the struggle continues*

*ikatlong bahagi · patuloy ang pakikibaka*

## Sometimes, the Heart Yearns for Mangoes

Sometimes, the heart yearns
For mangoes where there are apples,
For orchids where there are tulips,
For warmth, where it is cold,
For mountainous islands,
Where there is flatland.

Far less than the home,
And the flow of kith and kin,
Unfamiliar and now familiar
Things and places trigger
The pain of sundered relations,
Of losses by delays and default.

Direct dialing, fax machines,
Computer discs and video casettes
And visitors on jumbo jets,
Fail to close the gap
Between rehearsed appearances
And the unrehearsed life at home.

There are colleagues and friends
That make a strange land loveable.
But they have their routines,

## Minsa'y Sabik ang Puso sa Mangga

Kung minsan, sabik ang puso
Sa mangga kung saan may mansanas
Sa orkidya kung saan may tulipa
Sa init kung saan maginaw
Sa mabundok na kapuluan
Kung saan kapatagan.

Malayong kulang sa tahanan
At daloy ng kaibiga't kaanak
Di-gamay at ngayo'y gamay
Na mga bagay at lugar ay nang-uudyok
Ng kirot sa patid na mga ugnay,
Sa mga kabiguan dahil sa antala't kaligta.

Direct dialing, fax machine
Computer disc at video cassette
At mga bisitang lulan ng jet
Bigong paglapitin
Ang inensayong pamalas
At di-inensayong buhay sa tahanan.

May mga kaliga at kaibigan
Na nagpapaaya sa dinayong lupa
Subalit may sarili silang mga gawi,

Their own lives to live,
Beyond the comprehension
And pertinence of the stranger.

Those who seek to rob the exile
Of home, kith and kin,
Of life, limb and liberty
Are the loudest to mock at him
Who is helplessly at sea,
Uprooted from his soil.

The well-purposed exile continues
To fight for his motherland
Against those who banished him,
The unwelcomed exploiters of his people,
And is certain that he is at home
In his own country and the world.

*30 March 1994*

Sariling takbo ng mga buhay
Na lampas sa pagkaunawa
At kinalaman ng dayuhan.

Yaong mga nais magkait sa destiyero
Ng tahanan, kaibiga't kaanak,
Ng buhay, katawan at kalayaan
Ang pinakamaingay na mangutya sa kanya
Na lutang siya sa dagat,
Hugot ang ugat mula sa sariling lupa.

Patuloy ang may layuning destiyero
Na ipaglaban ang kanyang inangbayan
Laban sa mga nagpalayas sa kanya,
Ang mga inaayawang nagsasamantala sa bayan
At tiyak niyang siya'y nananahanan
Sa sariling bayan at sa sandaigdigan.

*30 Marso 1994*

## The Giant Oak
(Tribute to Comrade Mao Zedong)

In the bitterness of winter
The giant oak stands erect,
A hundred years old,
A tower of countless seasons.
The mayflies of summer
Are no match to the oak
And the merciless cold.

He who has departed
But whose spirit lives on
And cannot be exorcised
By all sorts of sorcerers
Is sometimes carved out
From a branch of the oak
In the image of his foes
For rituals to steal
The magic of his name.
There are the kisses of betrayal
On the parchment,
Droning incantations of sacrilege
And myths of infamy
Against his great memory.

Ang Higanteng Roble
(Parangal kay Kasamang Mao Zedong)

Sa tindi ng taglamig
Tuwid ang tindig ng higanteng roble
Sandaantaong gulang,
Tore ng di-mabilang na mga panahon.
Ang mga langaw ng tag-araw
Ay walang laban sa roble
At sa walang awang lamig.

Siyang pumanaw na
Subalit ang diwa'y buhay pa
At di kayang paalisin
Ng sarisaring manggagaway
Minsa'y nililok
Sa sanga ng roble
Kawangki ng kanyang mga katunggali
Sa mga ritwal para nakawin
Ang mahika ng kanyang ngalan.
May mga halik ng pagkakanulo
Sa pergamino,
Umuugong ng dalanging lapastangan
At mga alamat ng kasamaan
Laban sa dakila niyang alaala.

When foes are haunted
By his thoughts and deeds
They are in mortal fear
Of the living force inspired
For the bigger battles ahead,
As the light and darkness
Clash in the horizon
And as the best and the worst
Are driven to define themselves.

*26 December 1993*

Pag binabagabag ang mga kaaway
Ng kanyang diwa't gawa,
Sinasaklot sila ng takot
Sa buhay na lakas na pinasisigla,
Para sa mas malalaking labanan sa hinaharap,
Habang ang liwanag at dilim
Ay nagtutunggali sa abot-tanaw
At habang ang pinakamabuti at pinakamasama
Ay natutulak na maglahad ng sarili.

*26 Disyembre 1993*

Monsters in the Market
(Song Lyrics)

Shame on those who spread the false illusion
Of the free market and tout the law of the jungle.
The self-interest of monopolies is so visible,
A hand that squeezes and ruins the lives of people.

Monopolies are monsters preying on the market.
They can't hide their greed with any sleight of hand.
They make super-profits from the sweat and blood
Of entire nations, the workers and the peasants.

Awake and arise, unite to fight the monsters
That oppress and exploit the people
In the factories, farms and marketplace.
Let us free ourselves and build a new world.

They manipulate the prices of goods in the world.
Burden weaker countries with deficits and debts
And pay only a bit of the full value of labor power
And feed like sharks on the big unpaid labor.

Mga Halimaw sa Pamilihan
(Titik Awit)


Mahiya ang mga nagkakalat ng maling ilusyon
Ng libreng merkado at naglalako ng batas ng gubat.
Hantad ang makasariling interes ng mga monopolyo,
Kamay na pumipiga at sumisira sa buhay ng tao.

Mga monopolyo, halimaw na nandarambong sa pamilihan.
Kasakiman nila, di maitatago ng anumang salamangka.
Labis na tubo ang kuha nila sa pawis at dugo
Ng buo-buong bansa, manggagawa't magsasaka.

Gumising at tumindig, magkaisa't labanan ang halimaw
Na nang-aapi at nagsasamantala sa mga tao
Sa mga pagawaan, bukirin at palengke.
Sarili nati'y palayain at itayo ang bagong daigdig,

Minamanipula nila ang presyo ng mga kalakal sa mundo.
Pinapapasan sa mahihinang bayan ang depisit at utang,
Katiting ng halaga ng lakas paggawa ang binabayaran
At mala-pating, lamon ang malaking di-bayad na paggawa.

The imperialists plunder and unleash wars,
Gang up on weaker countries, nations and peoples
To rob them and curtail freedom
They rival and wrangle to re-divide the world.

Let us free ourselves and build a new world.

*December 2005*

Mga imperyalista'y nandarambong at nagpapakawala ng gera,
Pinagtutulungan ang mahihinang bayan, bansa't mamamayan
Upang nakawan sila at supilin ang kalayaan.
Nagriribal at nag-aaway sila sa muling pahahati ng mundo.

Sarili nati'y palayain at itayo ang bagong daigdig.

*Disyembre 2005*

The Way to a Just Peace
(Song Lyrics)

The Yanks came posing as a friend
Then they unleashed aggression
To rape, plunder and imprison
Our long suffering Motherland.
The way to a just peace is to fight
For national liberation

By ceaseless, ruthless use of arms
The ruling classes dominate,
Oppress and exploit the people
Mainly the workers and peasants.
The way to a just peace is to fight
For social liberation

The people must rise up to fight
The imperialists and puppets
Gain the power to free themselves
And build a just and lasting peace

The kind of peace that the imperialists
And the local exploiting classes wish
Is the abject surrender of the people
To the daily violence of exploitation.

Ang Daan sa Makatarungang Kapayapaan
(Titik-Awit)

Dumating ang mga Kano na umaastang kaibigan
Saka nagpakawala ng agresyon
Para gahasain, dambungin at ibilanggo
Ang matagal nang nagdurusang Inang-bayan.
Ang daan tungo sa makatarungang kapayapaan ay lumaban
Para sa pambansang pagpapalaya.

Sa walang humpay, malupit na paggamit ng armas
Nakakadomina ang mga naghaharing uri,
Nang-aapi at nagsasamantala sa sambayanan,
Pangunahin sa mga manggagawa at magsasaka.
Ang daan sa makatarungang kapayapaan ay lumaban
Para sa panlipunang pagpapalaya.

Dapat bumangon ang mamamayan para labanan
Ang mga imperyalista at mga papet
Kamtin ang kapangyarihang palayain ang sarili
At itayo ang makatarungan at matibay na kapayapaan.

Ang tipo ng kapayapaang nasa ng mga imperyalista
At lokal na mga nagsasamantalang uri
Ay ang abang pagsuko ng mga mamamayan
Sa araw-araw na karahasan ng pagsasamantala.

The way to a just peace is to end
The violence of exploitation .

The people must rise up to fight
The imperialists and puppets
Gain the power to free themselves
And build a just and lasting peace!

*December 2005*

Ang daan sa makatarungang kapayapaan ay wakasan
Ang karahasan ng pagsasamantala.

Dapat bumangon ang mamamayan para labanan
Ang mga imperyalista at mga papet
Kamtin ang kapangyarihang palayain ang sarili
At itayo ang makatarungan at matibay na kapayapaan!

*Disyembre 2005*

## The Charge against Me

So many times since a long time ago
Have I declared the obvious,
That the revolutionary leadership
Is in the Philippines and not abroad
And that I have neither power nor authority,
To order the acts of people's war.

The charge against me is false
And politically motivated,
Fabricated by a desperate regime
Out to silence me and all critics,
And hellbent on deflecting attention
From its howling violations
Of human rights in my country.

The charge is a bundle of malice,
Outright lies and half-truths
Hearsay and sheer speculations
Dished up to Dutch snoops
In a guided tour of malice
By the bloody rulers of my country.

No amount of reckless raids
On the houses and offices of Filipinos

## Ang Paratang sa Akin

Kay raming ulit sa mahabang panahon
Ipinahayag ko ang lantad na katunayan
Na ang rebolusyonaryong pamunuan
Ay nasa Pilipinas at hindi sa ibang bansa
At wala akong kapangyarihan o awtoridad,
Na iutos ang mga aksyon sa digmang bayan.

Ang paratang sa akin ay hindi totoo
At may pampulitikang pagdadadahilang,
Gawa-gawa ng desperadong rehimeng
Ang pakay ay patahimikin ako at lahat ng kritiko,
At malisyosong naglilihis ng pansin
Mula sa mga naghuhumiyaw na paglabag
Sa mga karapatang tao sa aking bansa.

Ang paratang ay isang bungkos na malisya,
Lantay na kasinungalingan at kalahating-katotohanan
Sabi-sabi at lantay na mga hakahaka
Na inihain sa mga tiktik na Olandes
Sa ginabayang lakbay ng malisya
Ng mga madugong naghahari sa aking bansa.

Kahit ilang barumbadong paglusob
Sa mga bahay at mga opisina ng mga Pilipino

And torturous interrogations
In my solitary confinement
Can make any more true
What is a false charge
In my ceaseless persecution.

*August 2007*

At mapamilit na mga interogasyon
Sa aking solitaryong pagkapiit
Hindi magagawang totoo nang kahit katiting
Ang huwad na paratang
Sa walang humpay na pang-uusig sa akin.

*Agosto 2007*

## Once More Solitary Confinement

At the peak of our youth,
Full of romance and vigor,
We were imprisoned for a long time
In a small and stifling cell
Of solitary confinement by the dictatorship
Where time was a turtle
As if we had no more hope
To be free from the steel door.

We were separated, my love.
And in extreme loneliness
My heart always cried out
That we come togethert again.
Loneliness and hope merged
In my fighting poems.
And in the long run, we came together
Upon the overthrow of the dictatorship.

Now that we are of mature age
Our resolve is ever more firm
But the body is fragile
And accustomed to your care
Once more I am imprisoned
In a small and stifling cell

# Bartolina Muli

Sa rurok ng ating kabataan,
Lipos ng pag-irog at sigla,
Malaon tayong ikinulong
Sa masikip at nakakasakal
Na bartolina ng diktadura
Kung saan usad-pagong ang panahon.
Wari'y wala na tayong pag-asang
Makalaya sa pintuang bakal.

Pinaghiwalay tayo hirang
At sa labis na pangungulila
Laging humihiyaw ang puso ko
Na magsiping muli tayo.
Nagsanib ang lungkot at pag-asa
Sa mga tula kong palaban.
At sa kalaunan, tayo'y nagsama
Sa paggapi sa diktadura.

Ngayong hinog na tayo sa gulang
Ibayong matibay ang kapasiyahan
Subalit marupok na ang katawan
At nahirati na sa iyong pagkalinga.
Ikinulong na naman ako
Sa masikip at nakakasakal

Of solitary confinement by the imperialists.
It looks like I will be finished here.

We are once more separared
And in extreme loneliness
My heart always cries out
Thhat we come together again
Loneliness and hope merge
In my fighting songs.
Let us be together again in the movement
And in fulfilling of our legacy to the people.

*August 2007*

Na bartolina ng mga imperyalista.
Waring dito na ako tatapusin .

Nagkawalay na naman tayo
At sa labis na pangungulila
Laging humihiyaw ang puso ko
Na magkasiping muli tayo.
Magkasanib ang lungkot at ligaya
Sa aking mga mapanlabang kanta.
Magsama muli tayo sa pagkilos
At sa paglulubos ng ating pamana sa bayan.

*Agosto 2007*

## Cry for Freedom

It used to be said
By my detractors
That I enjoy myself
In a haven of comfort
Dancing in opulence
Even as I was banned
From work, then deprived
of measly living allowance.

I am once more entombed
Buried alive in a cell
As in the years of Marcos.
Daily I suffer
The stifling walls,
The shut steel door
The spikes of insolence
And the spires of arrogance.

I am once more in hell,
Burning alive in a furnace,
By the direct hand of imperial powers,
Framing me up
Demonizing and mocking me,

## Isigaw ang Kalayaan

Dating ipinapahayag
Ng mga tagahamak sa akin
Na ako'y nagpapasarap
Sa kanlungan ng ginhawa
Sumasayaw sa karangyaan
Gayong ako'y pinagbawalang
Magtrabaho, saka pinagkaitan
Ng karampot na guguling pamuhay.

Ako ay muling inilagay sa nitso,
Inilibing na buhay sa isang selda
Tulad sa panahon ni Marcos.
Araw-araw pinagdurusa ako
Ng mga mapanikil na pader,
Ng pinid na pintong bakal.
Ng mga sima ng kawalang-galang
At ng sukdulang kapalaluan.

Ako ay muling nasa impiyerno,
Buhay na nasusunog sa isang pugon,
Tuwirang gawa ng mga imperyal na kapangyarihan,
Na nagpakana ng huwad na paratang
Pinag-iitsura akong demonyo at inaalipusta,

In a cold country
Away from home.

I must endure
The daily torture,
The anguish of innocence
Subjected to a false charge.
I can write poems,
I can sing songs,
I strive to breathe
And cry for freedom.

*4 September 2007*

Sa isang malamig na bayang
Malayo sa tahanan.

Dapat kong pangibabawan
Ang araw-araw na pagpapahirap,
Ang hinagpis ng kawalang-sala
Nilapatan ng huwad na paratang.
Maaari akong magsulat ng mga tula,
Maaari akong umawit ng mga kanta,
Pinagsisikapan kong huminga
At isigaw ang kalayaan.

*4 Setyembre 2007*

## The Inquisition

*Maximum Security Prison,\**
*Scheveningen, The Hague*

Every day without letup,
The inquisition goes on
In a cramped prison room
With the overheated bulb
On the ceiling cooking
My head and my brain.

Every day without let up,
The inquisition goes on,
With two questions repeated
And pressed into my ears:
Did you incite murder?
Do you head the people's army?

Everyday without letup,
The inquisition goes on.
I deny the charge.
I invoke the right
To remain silent
From beginning to end.
......

\* Former Nazi prison house and the Dutch Guantánamo.

Ang Ingkisisyon

> *Bilangguang Maximum Security,*
> *Scheveningen, The Hague*

Bawat araw walang puknat,
Patuloy ang ingkisisyon
Sa masikip na silid ng bilangguan,
Niluluto ng kay init na bombilya
Sa kisame sa tapat ko
 Ang aking ulo at utak.

Bawat araw walang puknat,
Patuloy ang ingkisisyon,
Dalawang tanong ang inuulit-ulit,
At idinidiin sa aking mga tainga:
Ikaw ba ang nag-udyok ng pagpaslang?
Ikaw ba ang namumuno sa hukbong bayan?

Bawat araw walang puknat,
Patuloy ang ingkisisyon.
Tinatanggihan ko ang paratang.
Iginigiit ko ang karapatang
Manatiling tahimik
Mula umpisa hanggang dulo.

Every day without let up,
The inquisition goes on.
The inquisitors are menacing
And assail me with lies,
Half-truths, insults,
Hearsay and speculation

Everyday without let up,
The inquisition goes on.
The drive is to force me
To incriminate myself
And finish me off
With the charge of terrorism.

Every day without let up,
The inquisition goes on.
I am pilloried in a series
Of lengthening detention orders
In order to bury me alive
And kill my voice.

But the people of the world
Are outraged by my ordeal
And stand up in solidarity
To defend and support me.
They struggle for justice.
Deeply I thank them.

*12 September 2007*

Araw-araw walang puknat,
Patuloy ang ingkisisyon,
Nananakot ang mga ingkisidor
At nanduduldol ng mga kasinungalingan,
Hating-katotohanan, insulto,
Sabi-sabi at haka-haka.

Bawat araw walang puknat,
Patuloy ang ingkisisyon,
Ang pakay ay pilitin ako
Na idawit ang sarili
At tapusin nila ako
Sa paratang ng terorismo.

Bawat araw walang puknat
Patuloy ang ingkisisyon
Ako ay iniipit sa isang serye
Ng papatagal na mando ng pagpiit
Upang ilibing nang buhay
At patayin ang aking tinig.

Ngunit ang mga mamamayan sa daigdig
Ay naaalipusta ng pahirap sa akin
At tumitindig para makipagkaisa
Upang ipagtanggol at tangkilikin ako.
Ipinaglalaban nila ang katarungan.
Taus-puso ko silang pinasasalamatan.

*12 Setyembre 2007*

## Demons in Two Domains

Acting on behalf of the Devil,
With the top hat and white beard,
Who glowers over the world
The demons in one domain
In my anguished motherland
Concoct certain incidents
As acts of terrorism
For which I am charged
To imprison my friends
And terrorize the nation.

Somehow the inspirited
And outraged people,
Who cherish and fight
for freedom and justice
In the beautiful islands,
Disprove and defeat the charge
And cast away the poisonous concoction
We are thus blessed
With a wise judgment
In one joyous shining moment.

Acting on behalf of the Devil,
With the top hat and white beard,

## Mga Demonyo sa Dalawang Dominyo

Kumikilos sa ngalan ng Dyablo
Na mataas ang sombrero at maputi ang balbas,
Lisik-matang tumitingin sa buong mundo,
Ang mga demonyo sa isang dominyo
Sa naghihinagpis kong inangbayan
Ay naglalang ng ilang pangyayari
Bilang mga akto ng terorismo
Na sa aki'y ipinaparatang
Upang ibilanggo ang mga kaibigan ko
At sindakin ang bansa.

Paanuman, ang pinasigla
At pinagngalit na mga mamamayan
Na nagmamahal at lumalaban
Para sa kalayaan at katarungan
Sa magandang kapuluan,
Ay pinabubulaanan at ginagapi ang mga paratang
At itinapon nila ang lasong gawa-gawa
Kaya kami ay pinagpala
Ng isang matinong hatol
Sa masayang maningning na sandali.

Kumikilos sa ngalan ng Dyablo,
Na mataas ang sombrero at maputi ang balbas,

Who glowers over the world,
The demons in another domain,
In a treacherous and false haven
Brew the same ingredients
As acts of murder
And charge me thus
To humiliate and imprison me
And terrify the world.

Somehow the inspired
And the rising people,
Who resist the evils
Of global greed and terror
Will someday prevail and defeat
The doubly baseless charge.
Discard the poisonous brew
And let freedom and justice
Triumph over imperial malice
Across the oceans.

*August 2007*

Lisik-matang tumitingin sa buong mundo,
Mga demonyo sa isa pang dominyo,
Sa mapagkanulo at huwad na kanlungan
Nagpakulo ng parehong mga sangkap
Bilang mga akto ng pagpaslang
At sa aki'y ipinaparatang
Upang hamakin at ibilanggo ako
At takutin ang buong mundo.

Paanuman, ang pinasigla
At bumabalikwas na mga mamamayan
Lumalaban sa kaimbihan
Ng buong mundong kasakiman at lagim.
Balang araw ay mananaig at gagapi
Sa dalawang ulit na walang-batayang paratang.
Itapon ang lasong gawa-gawa
At pagtagumpayin ang kalayaan at katarungan
Laban sa malisyang imperyal
Na tumatawid sa mga karagatan.

*Agosto 2007*

## My Pen and My Tongue

The only weapons I have
Are my pen and my tongue
To protest greed and terror
And call for people's resistance
In my Motherland and in the world.

I protest the daily violence
Of exploiting the toiling masses
And burying them in poverty,
Misery, slow death and silence.
I call for ending the pillage.

I protest the wars of aggression
And all acts of repression
That perpetuate exploitation
By the imperialists and puppets.
I call for ending the carnage.

I fight for justice and peace
In solidarity with all peoples
And I praise and encourage them
To wage the just struggle
For national and social liberation.

Aking Panulat at Dila

Ang tangi kong mga sandata
Ay aking panulat at ang aking dila
Upang tutulan ang kasakiman at lagim
At ipanawagan ang paglaban ng mga mamamayan
Sa aking Inangbayan at sa daigdig.

Tinututulan ko ang araw-araw na karahasan
Ng pagsasamantala sa anakpawis
At pagbaon sa kanila sa karukhaan,
Paghihirap, dahan-dahang kamatayan at pagtahimik.
Nananawagan akong wakasan ang pandarambong.

Tinututulan ko ang mga digmang agresyon.
At lahat ng kilos na mapanupil
Na nagpapanatili sa pagsasamantala
Ng mga imperyalista at mga papet.
Nananawagan akong wakasan ang pangangatay.

Ipinaglalaban ko ang katarungan at kapayapaan
Sa pakikipagkaisa sa lahat ng mamamayan
At pinupuri ko't pinalalakas ang loob nila
Upang isagawa ang makatarungang pakikibaka
Para sa pambansa at panlipunang pagpapalaya.

The imperialists and the puppets
React to my pen and tongue
With false charges, demonization
And the iron fist of state power.
But I stand with the people.

*4 September 2007*

Ang mga imperyalista't mga papet
Gumaganti sa aking panulat at dila,
Gamit ang mga huwad na paratang, demonisasyon
At ang kamay na bakal ng kapangyarihang estado.
Ngunit nakikipanindigan ako sa sambayanan.

*4 Setyembre 2007*

## Rulers and Butchers

The rulers and butchers of my country
Rain bombs and artillery fire
To force more than a million
Peasants and indigenous people
Out of their homes and land
And make way for plantations,
Mines and all kinds of plunder.
They think they can do so with impunity

They have murdered, abducted
And tortured more than a thousand
Workers, peasants, women,
Students, teachers, lawyers,
Journalists, priests and pastors
To quell the people's resistance
And keep the reign of greed and terror
They think they can do so with impunity.

Before a single one of them
Can be brought to justice
The rulers and butchers of my country
Have colluded with the imperialists
To put me once more in solitary,
As in the days of the Marcos tyranny,

## Mga Naghahari at Mangangatay

Ang mga naghahari at mangangatay ng aking bayan
Nagpapaulan ng mga bomba at artileriya
Upang pilitin ang higit sa isang milyong
Mga magsasaka at katutubo
Na umalis sa kanilang mga tahanan at lupain
At bigyan daan ang mga plantasyon,
Minahan at lahat ng klaseng pandarambong.
Akala nilang magagawa ito nang walang parusa.

Pinagpapapaslang, pinagdudukot
At pinahirapan ang higit sa isang libong
Mga manggagawa, magsasaka, kababaihan,
Mga mag-aaral, guro, abogado,
Mga mamamahayag, mga pari at pastor
Upang sugpuin ang paglaban ng mga mamamayan
At panatilihin ang paghahari ng kasakiman at lagim.
Akala nilang magagawa ito nang walang parusa.

Bago magawaran ng katarungan
Ang kahit isa man lang sa kanila
Ang mga naghahari at mga mangangatay ng aking bayan
Ay kakutsaba ng mga imperyalista
At inilagay ako muli sa solitaryo,
Tulad ng sa mga araw ng tiranya ni Marcos,

On a false charge of murder
For the revolutionary acts of the people.

I join the ranks of the victims
And I follow the examples
Of Ka Bel, Ka Satur, La Liza,
Ka Paeng, Ka Ted and Ka Joel
Persecuted but unbowed
By the oppressors and their foreign masters
Standing up for the just cause
Of the suffering and struggling people.

*7 September 2007*

Sa huwad na paratang ng pamamaslang
Para sa mga rebolusyonaryong kilos ng mga mamamayan.

Kasama ako sa hanay ng mga biktima
At sinusunod ko ang mga halimbawa
Nina Ka Bel, Ka Satur, La Liza,
Ka Paeng, Ka Ted at Ka Joel
Inaapi ngunit hindi yumuyuko
Sa mga mapang-api at mga banyagang amo nila,
Naninidigan sila para sa makatarungang adhikain
Ng mga nagdurusa at nakikibakang mamamayan.

*7 Setyembre 2007*

## Stages of My Life

If you trace the course
And the stages of my life,
The story is quite simple,
Easy to recall with the head and heart.

In the spring of my life,
I observed the hardship
Of the toiling masses around.
My heart and spirit was moved.

In the summer of my life,
I decided to fight
The oppressors and exploiters.
I was tempered in the flames of struggle.

In the autumn of my life,
I can see the wide scope
And the strong advance
Of the masses on fertile soil.

In the winter of my life,
I always feel from the field
The flames of struggle.
I am sure of the victory of the people.

*September 2007*

## Mga Yugto ng Buhay Ko

Kung babaybayin mo ang takbo
At mga yugto ng buhay ko,
Simple lang ang kwento,
Madaling isaulo at isapuso.

Sa tagsibol ng buhay ko,
Nasaksihan ko ang kahirapan
Ng anakpawis sa paligid.
Naantig ang aking puso't diwa.

Sa tag-init ng buhay ko,
Nagpasya akong lumaban
Sa mga mapang-api at mapagsamantala.
Pinanday ako sa alab ng pakikibaka.

Sa taglagas ng buhay ko,
Tanaw ko ang lawak
At malakas na pagsulong
Ng masa sa matabang lupa.

Sa taglamig ng buhay ko,
Dama ko lagi sa larangan
Ang apoy ng pakikibaka.
Tiyak ko ang tagumpay ng bayan.

*Setyembre 2007*

## How Filipinos Forget the Unforgiveable

Why wonder that many Filipinos
Forget that the US aggressors
Killed more than 1.5 million of them
To conquer and pacify the nation,
Rob it of its independence and wealth?

Filipinos forget the unforgivable
Precisely because the success of carnage
Has allowed the aggressor to appear
As the benefactor in peaceful assemblies,
In schools, churches, theatres and mass media.

The successful aggressors misrepresent
The exploitation and oppression of the people
As development and justify the superprofits
While they enjoy the assistance of puppets
In oppressing and exploiting the people.

The number of victims in the imperialist crime
Becomes more abstract as time rolls on
And the successful aggressors always preach
To the generations of victims that it is better
To stay in the cage than dare to struggle.

Paano Nalilimutan ng mga Pilipino
ang Di-Mapapatawad


Bakit pagtatakhan na maraming Pilipino
Ay nakalilimot na mga agresor na Amerikano
Ang pumaslang sa higit sa 1,500,000 sa kanila
Upang lupigin at payapain ang bansa,
Pagnakawan ng kanyang kasarinlan at kayamanan?

Nakakalimot ang Pilipino sa di-mapapatawad
Dahil nga sa matagumpay na pangangatay
Na nagpapahintulot sa agresor na umasta
Bilang tagapagpala sa mapayapang mga pagtitipon,
Sa mga paaralan, simbahan, sinehan at masmidya.

Nanlilinlang ang matagumpay na mga agresor
Na ang pagsasamantala't pang-aapi sa sambayanan
Ay kaunlaran at nagbibigay katwiran sa labis na tubo
Habang nakikinabang sa tulong ng mga papet
Sa pang-aapi at pagsasamantala sa mga mamamayan.

Ang bilang ng mga biktima sa imperyalistang krimen
Ay lalong nagiging abstrakto sa paggulong ng panahon
At laging nangangaral ang matagumpay na manlulusob
Sa mga salinlahi ng mga biktima na mas mahusay
Manatili sa hawla kaysa mangahas lumaban.

The unforgiveable is not really forgettable
When revolutionary forces persevere
In arousing, organizing and mobilizing
The people to remember the blood debt
And struggle for national and social liberation.

*August 2013*

Di naman talaga malilimutan ang di-mapapatawad
Kapag magtiyaga ang mga rebolusyonaryong pwersa
Sa paghimok, pag-organisa at pagpapakilos
Sa mga mamamayan upang tandaan ang dugong inutang
At ipaglaban ang pambansa at panlipunang pagpapalaya.

*Agosto 2013*

## The Master Puppeteer and the Puppets

In neocolonial times, the master puppeteer
Lends the puppets grandeur and puts them
On the stage, in the mass media, all sorts of gatherings.
To conjure the illusion of democracy, he arranges
The electoral contests like dazzling cock fights
In so many town fiestas for several months.

But most important to the master puppeteer
Is to elect the puppet politicians that serve best
The collaboration of the US and local exploiters,
And make the exploited and oppressed believe
That they have freely chosen the best of possible.
Thus, the US has prolonged its domination.

But the revolutionary movement has arisen
To arouse, organize and mobilize the masses,
To confront the oppressors and exploiters,
To seize power wave upon wave in the localities
And gain strength for the liberation of the nation
And mainly the workers and peasants.

## Ang Maestro ng Titiretero at mga Papet

Sa panahong neokolonyal, ang maestrong titiretero
Ay pinahihiram ng dingal ang mga papet at ilinalagay
Sa entablado, sa masmidya at sari-saring pagtitipon.
Upang likhain ang ilusyon ng demokrasya, inaayos niya
Ang elektoral na paligsahan tulad ng makulay na sabungan
Sa kay raming pista ng bayan sa ilang buwan.

Ngunit ang pinaka-mahalaga sa maestrong titiretero
Ay piliin ang mga pulitikong papet na pinakalistong maglingkod
Sa kolaborasyon ng US at mga lokal na nagsasamantala,
At papaniwalain ang mga pinagsamantalahan at inaapi
Na sila ang malayang pumili sa posibleng pinakamahusay.
Sa gayon, napapatagal ng US ang kanyang pagdomina.

Ngunit bumangon ang rebolusyonaryong kilusan
Upang pukawin, organisahin at pakilusin ang masa
Upang harapin ang mga nang-aapi at nagsasamantala,
Upang agawin nang paalon-alon ang poder sa mga lokalidad
At kamtin ang lakas para sa pagpapalaya ng bansa
At pangunahin ang mga manggagawa at magsasaka.

The Filipino people shun the master puppeteer
For rotating puppet rulers to oppress them,
They reject the blatant despotism of Marcos
As well as the pseudo-democratic successors
Who take turns at oppressing the people
And serving the foreign and local exploiters.

*August 2013*

Suklam ang sambayanang Pilipino sa maestro titiretero
Sa pagpapalit-palit ng pinunong papet upang apihin sila,
Tinatanggihan nila ang garapal na despotismo ni Marcos
Gayundin ang mga huwad na demokratikong kasunod
Na naghahalinhinan sa pang-aapi sa sambayanan
At naglilingkod sa dayuhan at lokal na mga mapagsamantala.

*Agosto 2013*

## The Monster Ravages the Forests and Mountains

The birds have fled and sing no more
Where the monster has felled the trees
With complete abandon, with no concern
For the life of the forest that he ravages.

The wooden furniture and panelings
Of homes and offices in cities are splendid
While the folks where the trees are gone
Miss the savor of wild plants and animals.

And the flood and drought take turns
In drowning and parching the land
To ruin the rhythm and future of crops
And afflict the folks in the valleys and plains.

The monster is frenzied at ripping off
The mineral ores from the mountains.
He digs wide open pits and uses chemicals
Of the deadliest sorts to hasten the extraction.

## Sinasalanta ng Halimaw ang mga Gubat at Bundok

Lumikas ang mga ibon at hindi na umaawit
Kung saan itinumba ng halimaw ang mga puno
Nang walang pakundangan, walang malasakit
Sa buhay ng gubat na sinasalanta niya.

Napakainam ng mga kahoy na muebles at panel
Ng mga tahanan at tanggapan sa lungsod
Habang ang mga tao kung saan nawalan ng mga puno
Napagkaitan ng linamnam ng ligaw na halaman at hayop.

At halinhinan ang baha at tuyot
Sa paglunod at pagtigang sa lupa
Upang sirain ang ritmo at kinabukasan ng mga pananim
At papagdusahin ang mga tao sa mga lambak at patag.

Ulol na hinahablot ng halimaw
Ang mga sangkap na mineral mula sa mga bundok.
Nagdudukal ng malalawak na hukay at gumagamit ng mga kemikal
Na pinakamabagsik upang mapabilis ang paghango.

The monster is pleased with the gold,
Silver, platinum, nickel, chrome, zink, copper
And other ores to feed his industry
And make all sorts of strong and shiny things,

While poison flows to the streams and wells,
The tailings silt and choke the rivers,
And the mountains erode until they crumble
With landslides and mud flows to afflict the folks.

By denuding the forests, the monster robs
The land of its lungs and the shield against typhoons.
By extracting the ores, he robs the country
Of its development independent of its greed.

*August 2013*

Ang halimaw ay nasisiyahan sa ginto,
Pilak, platino, nikel, kromo, zinc, tanso
At iba pang sangkap para ipalamon sa kanyang industriya
At yumari ng lahat ng matibay at makintab na bagay,

Habang dumadaloy ang lason sa mga sapa at bubon,
Ang mga labi ng minahan ay naiipon at bumabara sa mga ilog
At ang mga bundok naaagnas hanggang malusaw
Upang pagdusahin ang mga tao sa mga guho ng putik at bato.

Sa pagkalbo sa mga gubat, ninanakaw ng halimaw
Ang baga ng lupa at ang kalasag nito laban sa mga unos.
Sa paghango ng mga mineral, ninanakaw sa bansa
Ang pag-unlad na malaya sa kanyang kasakiman.

*Agosto 2013*

## US Is the Terrorist Monster

The US has not yet paid for the blood debt
In killing 1.5 million of the Filipino people
And has not cared to give even an apology
As it continues to violate their sovereignty
And enjoy the bounty of successful aggression
And treachery with impunity and utmost arrogance.

The Filipino people have suffered the terrorism
Of US imperialism for so long, as if without end,
And with the help of its puppet accomplices,
It designates as terrorist and further represses
The victims and the revolutionary forces
Who fight for national and social liberation.

Empires have come and gone in history.
US imperialism and capitalism are not eternal.
The people strive to undercut and topple
The power of the system that oppresses them.
The people cannot accept the terrorist monster
Maligning as terrorist their heroes and forces.

*August 2013*

## US ang Teroristang Halimaw

Hindi pa nagbabayad ang US sa inutang na dugo
Sa pagpaslang ng 1.5 milyong mamamayang Pilipino
At hindi pa humihingi ng patawad man lamang
Habang patuloy na lumalabag sa kanilang soberanya
At nagtatamasa ng biyaya sa matagumpay na agresyon
At kataksilang walang parusa at sukdulang kapalaluan.

Nagdurusa ang sambayanang Pilipino sa terorismo
Ng imperyalismong US nang kay tagal na, wari'y walang hanggan,
At sa tulong ng mga papet na kasabwat,
Itinuturing bilang mga terorista at lalo pang sinusupil
Ang mga biktima at pwersang rebolusyonaryo
Na lumalaban para sa pambansa at panlipunang paglaya.

Sumusulpot at naglalaho ang mga imperyo sa kasaysayan.
May katapusan din ang imperyalismong US at kapitalismo.
Pinagsisikapan ng sambayanan na pahinain at igupo
Ang kapangyarihan ng sistemang nang-aapi sa kanila.
Hindi matatanggap ng bayan ang paninira ng teroristang halimaw
Na tawaging terorista ang kanilang mga bayani at pwersa.

*Agosto 2013*

## The Bells of Balangiga

In unison with the clear signal,
The pealing of the bells of Balangiga,
The outcry for struggle and freedom
Resounded in the breasts of the people.
The entire people rose up
And sallied forth against the alien monster,
Against the occupation and seizure
Of the freedom of their beloved country.

The monster decided to destroy
All the communities,
Burned down the homes,
Herded the people like animals,
Tortured and murdered
The menfolk and the children,
Raped the women,
Insulted the aged.

He climbed the tower
And stole the bells of Balangiga,
Carried it across the ocean
To imprison these in a fort
In the innermost recesses of the empire
To boast of them as trophies

## Mga Batingaw ng Balangiga

Sa pagkalembang, hudyat na malinaw,
Ng mga batingaw ng Balangiga,
Sa dibdib ng bayan umalingawngaw
Ang nasang lumaban at lumaya.
Sinugod ang banyagang halimaw
Ng taumbayang nagbalikwas
Laban sa pananakop at pag-agaw
Sa kalayaan ng mahal na bayan.

Ang halimaw nagpasyang manira
Sa lahat ng pamayanan,
Sinunog ang mga tahanan,
Tinipong parang hayop ang mga tao
Pinahirapan at pinaslang
Ang kalalakihan pati mga bata,
Ginahasa ang kababaihan
Dinusta ang matatanda.

Inakyat at kinulimbat mula sa tore
Ang mga batingaw ng Balangiga,
Itinawid sa malawak na karagatan
Upang bihagin ang sa kuta
Sa pinakapusod ng imperyo.
Ipagmalaking mga tropeo

Of the pillage of another country
And contempt for its independence.

Generations have passed
And the bells remain
As prisoners across the ocean.
The imperialists wish to silence their sound
But they are always thundering,
Resounding in the hearts and minds
Of the people continuing in struggle
For their freedom.

*9 August 2009*

Ng pagdambong sa ibang bayan
At paglapastangan sa kasarinlan nito.

Ilang salinlahi na ang nagdaan
At nananatili ang mga batingaw
Bilang bihag sa ibayong dagat.
Nais sikilin ng imperyalista ang tunog
Subalit lagi itong umuugong,
Umaalingaw sa puso't diwa
Ng taumbayang patuloy sa pakikibaka
Para sa kanilang kalayaan.

*9 Agosto 2009*

## Tribute to Comrade Andres Bonifacio

How great was Comrade Andres Bonifacio?
He did not believe as sacred and eternal
The colonial and feudal bastion of greed and terror.
He detested the collusion of sword and cross,
He trusted the entire people could prevail
If they dared to unite and fight the oppressor.

How pure was Comrade Andres Bonifacio?
He decided to serve the people
To fight for national independence,
Achieve justice and progress.
He offered his life and was to ready to die
For the people and for their bright future.

How brilliant was Comrade Andres Bonifacio?
He drew knowledge from history
And the condition of the working people
Who suffered, strove and hoped to free themselves
From exploitation and oppression
By the greedy and cruel foreign and local masters.

How learned was Comrade Andres Bonifacio?
More than those who reached the university
Who did not know or care to know the anguish

## Parangal Kay Ka Andres Bonifacio

Gaano kadakila si Ka Andres Bonifacio?
Hindi siya naniwala na banal at palagian
Ang kolonyal at pyudal na muog ng sakim at lagim.
Suklam siya sa sabwatan ng espada at krus.
May tiwala siyang mananaig ang sambayanan
Pag nagkaisa't nangahas lumaban sa mang-aapi.

Gaano kadalisay si Ka Andres Bonifacio?
Nagpasya siyang maglingkod sa bayan
Para ipaglaban ang pambansang kalayaan,
Kamtin ang katarungan at kaunlaran.
Nag-alay ng buhay at handang mamatay
Para sa bayan at maaliwalas nilang kinabukasan.

Gaano katalino si Ka Andres Bonifacio?
Hango ang kaalaman sa kasaysayan
At kalagayan ng masang anakpawis
Na nagdusa, nagsikap at umasang makalaya
Sa pagsasamantala at pang-aapi ng mga among
Dayuhan at lokal na ganid at malupit.

Gaano karunong si Ka Andres Bonifacio?
Higit pa sa mga nakapagpamantasan
Na walang alam o pakialam sa hinagpis

Of the toiling masses and what they can do.
More than those who neither read nor understood
The spirit of liberty, equality and fraternity.

How valiant was Comrade Andres Bonifacio?
He built the Katipunan in the face of intimidation
With the arrest of Rizal and dismantling of the Liga.
He was resolved to break the chains of colonial rule,
He declared independence and led the revolution.
Thus, he became the Father of the Filipino nation.

How worthy was Comrade Andres Bonifacio?
Rizal lacked trust in the revolution and the masses
And spurned the earnest offer for him to lead.
Miong seized the leadership and slew the Supremo.
The honor of the martyr hero shines forever
Against treason and repeated surrender to the foe.

How further worthy was Comrade Andres Bonifacio?
The revolution he led opened the road
Of democratic revolution in the whole of Asia.
Thus, the honor of Bonifacio rose so high
Towards the leadership of his proletarian class
In the era of the new-democratic revolution .

Comrade Andres Bonifacio remains our inspiration,
His example is always our guide
Our urgent task to emulate him and advance
What he began until we achieve complete victory.

Ng mga anakpawis at sa kung ano ang kaya nila.
Higit pa sa mga di nagbasa o di nakasapol
Sa diwa ng kalayaan, kapantayan at kapatiran.

Gaano kagiting si Ka Andres Bonifacio?
Itinayo ang Katipunan sa kabila ng pananakot
Sa paghuli kay Rizal at pagbuwag sa Liga.
May pasyang lagutin ang tanikalang kolonyal
Ihayag ang kasarinlan at pamunuan ang rebolusyon.
Sa gayon, naging Ama ng bansang Pilipino.

Gaano kahalaga si Ka Andres Bonifacio?
Kulang sa tiwala si Rizal sa rebolusyon at masa
At tinanggian ang dibdibang alok na mamuno.
Pamunua'y inagaw ni Miong at pinaslang ang Supremo.
Laging nagniningning ang dangal ng bayaning martir
Laban sa kataksilan at maulit na pagsuko sa kalaban.

Gaano pa kahalaga si Ka Andres Bonifacio?
Ang pinamunuan niyang rebolusyon ang nagbukas
Ng landas ng demokratikong rebolusyon sa buong Asya.
Kaya, napakataas ng karangalan ni Bonifacio
Tungo sa pamumuno ng kanyang uring proletaryo
Sa panahon ng bagong demokratikong rebolusyon.

Patuloy na inspirasyon natin si Ka Andres Bonifacio,
Patnubay natin ang kanyang halimbawa.
Mahigpit nating tungkuling tularan siya at isulong
Ang sinimulan niya hanggang ganap na ipagtagumpay.

Fight to defeat imperialism and reaction,
Achieve freedom and move towards socialism.

*26 August 2013*

Lumaban upang gapiin ang imperyalismo at reaksyon,
Kamtin ang kalayaan at tumungo sa sosyalismo.

*26 Agosto 2013*

*fourth part · commentaries*

# Literary Craft and Commitment

There are times when the poet seems to be struck by the afflatus. And he can compose the entire poem in a trice, as if the lines were in cadence with an accelerated heartbeat and came rushing, outracing the mind or the hand.

There are times when a single felt idea, image or metaphor, a mytho-pattern, a singing line or two, or some other element or fragment of the prospective poem ignites the whole creative process and soon results in at least a rough draft that takes so little effort to polish.

Is writing poetry so facile? No. And it is not only because most poems, which are well unified and precise in so many respects, obviously involve the disciplined use of skills in a difficult craft. The surges of "inspiration" are the result of prolonged and intense concentration of the poet in a special field of subjectivity – that of the poetic imagination, the most acute form of combining thought and feeling.

We assume here that to be mature and serious the poet has undergone a long and deepgoing process of arriving at a world outlook, enriching his life through personal experience and collective practice with others, mastering the language and learning from the literary masters and all along developing his own skills in the craft. But to create poems, the poet has to operate in the field of the poetic imagination constantly or at the least for extended periods of time.

The muse of poetry is demanding and jealous. She abandons the poet if he is not devoted enough and he takes on some other preoccupying tasks. That is the reason why poets in the Philippines die or fade away when they become full-time journalists, advertising copywriters, teachers, clerks, politicians, or what else. The present society in the Philippines does not allow many poets to live on poetry.

\*

I think that great literature in different ages in the world and the major works so far written in Philippine literary history assume significance, social and cultural, insofar as they are somehow committed to the cause of freedom and they reflect with profound insights the social conditions and the struggle for greater freedom.

It is on the basis of solid historical proof that I urge all Filipino creative writers to commit their minds, hearts and works to the struggle for freedom. Their works cannot but gain significance by reflecting, enriching and inspiring their people's struggle for national freedom and democracy in the present semicolonial and semifeudal society. Literature must serve the people more effectively than ever before.

The most vital issues and conflicts in society are crying out to be concentrated, represented and resolved in literary works. The people are suffering from fascist tyranny the bitter fruit of foreign and feudal domination – in a rapidly worsening political and economic crisis; and they are valiantly rising up to assert their national and democratic rights and fight for their freedom.

For the Filipino creative writers today, there can be no richer source of themes and raw materials than the sharpening struggle between reaction and revolution. There can be no better way to push forward the cause of freedom in Philippine literature than to deal with the decline of the present social system and the growth of the people's revolutionary struggle for freedom.

When I refer to the people, I mean the toiling masses of workers and peasants and such other democratic forces as the urban petty bourgeoisie and the national bourgeoisie. From among these classes there is one that provides the correct or best possible vantage point for creative writers.

I mean the working class, it is not only the productive vanguard for industrialization and modernization but it is also the basis for the most progressive world outlook and methodology for comprehending all social forces and their development in the current national democratic revolution as well as in the subsequent socialist revolution.

The revolutionary liberalism of the patriotic section of the bourgeoisie runs next to the proletarian ideology in importance and efficacy so long as both ideologies are in alliance. As amply proven since the defeat of the old democratic revolution, revolutionary liberalism can no longer take the lead in the resurgence of the Philippine revolution. Standing alone, revolutionary liberalism cannot defeat pro-imperialist liberalism, which is the official ideology of the big comprador-landlord state.

It is of great and decisive advantage for the Filipino creative writers to adopt the proletarian standpoint It allows them to comprehend the economic, political and cultural aspects of society and to know incisively the basic facts and trends in a number of contradictions: between the forces and relations of production; between the exploited and exploiting classes; between the state and the people; and between reactionary and revolutionary culture.

The proletarian creative writer understands comprehensively and profoundly the objective social reality and becomes a revolutionary partisan in the great struggle for freedom, justice and progress. Intellectually, he surpasses the individualistic, narrow and fragmentary knowledge of the unremoulded petty bourgeois intellectual and, of course, the far more outmoded ideas and values of the feudal past.

But it is one thing to adopt the correct and progressive intellectual and political outlook. It is another thing to create excellent literary works. The literary craft requires the literary or artistic imagination. This involves not only thought but the special unity of thought and feeling; content and form; subject and style; and so on.

To create significant works, the proletarian creative writer has the advantage of grasping the typical from diffuse social reality through investigation and analysis. But he has the burden, as all creative writers of whatever standpoint have to give concrete and sensuous life to the typical or conceptual in an imaginative way.

The basic stuff of the creative writer is the word as it is denotative and connotative. The literary forms and devices enhance both thought and feeling, and yet restrain them to make for precision, subtlety and beauty. There is a sense of spontaneity in all literary forms but there is also a sense of discipline required by the theme and its development.

The literary essay is the most explicit in the handling of thought through points and counterpoints even as a great deal of feeling is carried by concrete observations. The sensuousness of human experience and also subtlety increase in prose fiction and the drama because of the interplay and conflicts of characters as well as within characters. There is the tension of more feeling and thought put into less words in poetry although the long poem is more explicit in thought than the short poem.

Creative writing is a highly subjective activity, combining thought and feeling. It is among the finest and highest product of human consciousness. It is an important component of the cultural sphere which is above but not detached from the economic and political spheres. And culture both reflects and interacts with both economics and politics.

Proletarian creative writing reflects best at this point in history the social conditions, struggles and aspirations of the people, especially the toiling masses of workers and peasants. At the same time, it inspires and helps clarify the revolutionary course of the people. It puts forward heroes and noble ideas from the common people and revolutionaries who are either underrated, ignored or opposed by nonproletarian creative writers.

In the Philippines today, bourgeois creative writing has two major categories of writers: the revolutionary liberal and pro-imperialist liberal. Proletarian creative writers appreciate the critical realism and the scientific and democratic tendencies of revolutionary liberal works. But, of course, both proletarian and revolutionary liberal creative writers oppose the utterly reactionary content of pro-imperialist liberal works, even if the style is distinguishably excellent.

The propaganda of "art for art's sake" is nothing but a minor excrescence of bourgeois subjectivism and pro-imperialist liberalism, no matter how hard it claims to be detached from any class, engages in psychological self-titillation, retails anecdotes of political ignorance and cynicism or makes abrupt mystical flights from the level of instinct and ego. The slogan of "art for art's sake" and the works that come under it are manifestations of the self-indulgence of some unremoulded petty bourgeois writers.

The possibility of creative writing from a proletarian revolutionary viewpoint started in 1930, when Marxism started to take roots in the Philippines. With varying degrees of success, some proletarian literary works were written in the thirties and early forties. But from the later 1950s onwards, in a crescendo conspicuously seen in the seventies and now in the eighties, such works have made a resurgence. These include the works of the late Amado V. Hernandez and many of the young creative writers today.

Proletarian creative writing inherits the people's collective spirit in folk literature; the critical realism in Balagtas' allegorical romance, *Florante at Laura*; the criticism of social structure and manners and the anti-colonial and democratic thrust of Rizal's *Noli Me Tangere* and *El Filibusterismo* and his essays;

the patriotic spirit in anti-US plays during the early years of US colonial rule; and also the critical realism and democratic spirit in short stories, novels and poems in all the decades that have passed in the twentieth century.

As the people's revolutionary movement grows and advances, proletarian creative writers are bound to increase their literary output in all forms and raise its aesthetic quality from one level to another. Their standpoint, themes, heroes, plots and direction evoke the acute interest of the largest possible readership and audience – the working people.

The use of the national language plays a decisive role in stimulating both proletarian literary activity and the interest of the masses in proletarian literary works; and in isolating the diehard pro-imperialist liberal and other reactionary creative writers who wish to perpetuate their literary theory and tastes derived from reactionary bourgeois books in English as a result of US cultural domination.

The total victory of the national democratic revolution will guarantee the predominance of a national, scientific and mass culture and the most favorable conditions for the further growth of proletarian creative writing.

– Jose Ma. Sison
Political Prisoner
Military Security Command
Fort Bonifacio
1983

## Beyond Transcendence, Toward Incarnation: The Poetry of Jose Ma. Sison

> *Piita'y bahagi ng pakikilamas,*
> *mapiit ay tanda ng hindi pagsuko...*
> *tanang paninil ay may pagtutuos,*
> *habang may Bastilya'y may bayang gaganti.*
> – Amado V. Hemandez, "Isang Dipang Langit"

When I visited London in the summer of 1981 on my way back from Yugoslavia where I chaired a post-graduate seminar in Third World poetics, I had the fortuitous occasion to talk to the Asian editor of Index, a European Journal devoted to exposing and indicting press censorship and assisting persecuted writers anywhere in the world. I then conceived myself the bearer of messages from home. Despite my impassioned effort to convince the editor to publicize the brutal, inhuman punishment being inflicted on Jose Ma. Sison by the Marcos regime, the simple and naive retort I got was: Sison is in prison not as a writer but as a revolutionary partisan, an organizer of armed struggle.

From the Westernized perception of an Asian exile, Sison's writings are incidental, even accidental, to his revolutionary calling. Whereas Index, given its aristocratic bias, privileges the fulltime artisan of the Word whose craft happens, by circumstance or sheer bad luck, to have incurred the ire of the authorities. Thus, Sison the radical exponent of the national democratic cause would not qualify. I dared a riposte: "But surely Byron, Malraux, Ho Chi Minh, Neruda…" But in the milieu of a fragmented and commodified metropolis, the fortress of a moribund empire where the centuries-old ideology of reification still reigns supreme, my plea for upholding the old bourgeois illusion of the total integrated person – of Sison as an artist and revolutionary evaporated in the pollution and cacophony of London traffic.

It is now the close of 1982, marking ten years of martial law and also ten years of popular resistance. This all-embracing dialectical unity of opposites informing our national development finds its poignant emblem in one of Sison's latest poems, "The Forest Is Still Enchanted" [40].* While the disintegrating feudal cosmos of superstition and natural abundance (an ironic figure given the rabid transnational plunder of our resources) inevitably yields to the World Bank-funded infrastructures and to the electronics counter-insurgency apparatus, still the element of awe and the new, now displaced as a trope of the people's will to resist alienating and exploitative forces, persists.

*But the forest is still enchanted.*
*There is a new hymn in the wind;*
*There is a new magic in the dark green,*
*So the peasant folks say to friends.*
*A single fighting spirit has taken over*
*To lure in and astonish the intruders.*

──────
* Page numbers between square brackets refer to the present volume.

The understated allusion, of course, is to the peasantry's allegiance to the New People's Army and the prairie-fire resurgence of people's war. But what is striking here is the coalescence of myth and history – already prefigured in "The Guerrilla Is Like a Poet" [24], "From a Burning Bush" [48], etc. – which, I submit, defines the essentially prophetic thrust and vocation of Sison's linguistic practice, a praxis whose visionary mission is to simultaneously demystify the alienated world and project images of apocalyptic rebirth.

From the view of traditional hermeneutics, this prophetic impulse which transforms linear time to kaleidoscopic space, memory into action, and in the process enacts a creative dialogue between spirit and matter, can be explained by Sison's confinement and the claustrophobic syndrome coinciding with it, as evinced, for instance, in Gramsci's motto: "Pessimism of the mind, optimism of the will." Pursuing this trend, one can plausibly analogize the theme of such poems as "In the Dark Depths" [94], "A Furnace" [102], and others, with Sison's litany of suffering and anguished privations distilled, for example, in his May 1982 Statement (Political Detainees Update): "Our prolonged solitary confinement has cumulatively increased the intensity of our imprisonment so much so that we have in effect suffered by so many times the bare number of five and six years that we have already spent in prison."

It might be more appropriate, however, to reflect on the idea that subsuming the personal or biographical context, the raw materials worked on by a rigorously dialectical mode of literary production, is precisely that sine qua non, the constellation of first principles, which at once incorporates critical realism, supersedes it, and elevates it to the level of prophetic allegory, proletarian ideology, dialectical materialism.

For this occasion, I will not elaborate on those first principles and will limit myself to emphasizing the crucial determining function of a Marxist-Leninist theoretical perspective in elucidating Sison's poetics. Contrary to the mistaken academic notion, this perspective is not a specialized "workerist" bias, or reductive economistic presumption. It is fundamentally a totalizing historical outlook without which one falls (as Lukács points out in *History and Class Consciousness*) into the dualistic chasms of abstract formalist idealism and of mechanical materialism. Sison himself, in his recent Message to the UP-Writers' Club (its intertextuality with his previous messages to PAKSA, LEADS, and also to the relevant chapters of Struggle for National Democracy needs to be explored) reformulates that proposition and urges progressive writers to leap beyond neocolonial liberalism and position themselves in the pregnant and fertile space occupied by the working class. Why? Because, to quote Sison, "It is not only the productive vanguard for industrialization and modernization but it is also the basis for the most progressive world outlook and methodology for comprehending all social forces and their development in the current national democratic revolution as well as in the subsequent socialist revolution."

Also synthesized by implication in Sison's message is the basic materialist principle of analyzing overdetermined contradictions: literary production as an instance of ideological practice cannot be divorced from the socio-economic formation, the entire oscillating totality within which it interacts with other regions as a relatively autonomous force. Hence, like Mao's strategic reminder in the 1942 Yenan Talks on literature and art, Sison also posits literary specificity (distinguished from the political or programmatic) as a tension between spontaneity vis a vis discipline, the private realm of feelings vis a vis the socializing effect of linguistic practice and the task of art to systematically humanize reality.

Such a distinction, however, reinforced by the arguments of Althusser and Gramsci, should not obscure the truth that all art springs and is nourished by human needs and passions that transpire in history. And its fabled transcendence of empirical contingency, the so-called universality of art, exists only because we, humans, resurrect, reincarnate and renew those once fluid energies now petrified in museum fetishes and gallery commodities: those living energies which, once unleashed in the "festival of the oppressed," begin to crystallize our hope and desire to change life (as Rimbaud and Rilke vowed to do) and thereby transform the world. Conceived then as the living science of praxis, i.e., the conscious and sensuous activity of the human species, poetry cannot but be politically/historically engaged.

To further underscore the primacy of the materialist framework, I quote Sison's concluding words in the WHO magazine interview (12 December 1981): "In sum I would say that my books are linked to the great tradition of the Philippine revolution and the mass movements of workers, peasants, urban petty bourgeoisie and other patriotic forces." Whether in 1896 (Rizal and the Propagandists), in the 1950s (Baking, Hernandez, Lansang) or today, the Filipino intellectual finds himself always already embedded, knowingly or unknowingly, in the compromising, recalcitrant "thickness" of class struggle; and to such a situation he can only respond in two mutually incompatible ways: by full commitment to the side of the progressive forces, or by temporizing ruses – the mirror-image of blatant collaboration with the fascist agents of US imperialism.

Isn't our history replete with the lessons of Biak-na-bato, with the ordeals of making a choice at those peaks of crises: the Filipino–American War, the Sakdalista uprising, the Huk rebellion, and now?

Given our historical predicament, the Filipino writer then finds himself "compromised" in both the pejorative and honorific senses, only because his practice of language, his processing of signs, occurs within a concrete, specific site of conflict which necessarily stakes his body and the bodies of his affections – a site within which is inscribed as in a constantly deciphered palimpsest the incandescent dynamics of hope evolving into will or personal desire unfolding in the matrix of a collective dream.

There is in Sison's corpus of poems no more eloquently moving and intransigently perspicuous testament to this materialist aesthetics I have sketched above than "The Bladed Poem." Here we perceive the two phases of the social process: workers objectively defined as functions within a commodity-oriented system, and workers emerging as the collective subject organized and cohering around a project of self-knowledge achieved only in revolution. We have then the worker depicted as the artificer of the social totality in motion in which labor metamorphoses into play, the play of struggle, in which they experience the pleasurable release and fulfillment of needs and phantasies. Art is then grasped as both a pedagogical instrument (a learning tool, Brecht would say) and a weapon of organizing.

So far we have moved from the romanticized equation of the earlier "The Guerrilla Is Like a Poet" to the imaginative fusion of theory and practice, consciousness and action, in the prison poems where the symbols and archetypes of freedom are glimpsed presaging its eventual conquest in real life. Sison's poems are thus incomplete, denied organic closure, because the materialist textualization of struggle escapes from the prison-house of language in order to emancipate itself in the discourse of physical combat.

In an essay I wrote for an *UGNAYAN* pamphlet (1979) designed to publicize Sison's case to an international audience, I tried to articulate the nature of the prophetic or utopian motivation in Sison's poetics, in these terms: "Life is not a natural phenomenon governed by implacable laws. It is, for Sison and other Third World militants, a project shaped by, and shaping history. The solidarity of human wills, the fusion of participating subjects in organized action, intervenes in the world to create the groundwork for the future: a new society and culture that is genuinely popular, democratic, libertarian." I use the word "utopian" in the sense of Ernst Bloch's "hope principle": an apocalyptic gesture of precipitating the resolution of crisis (here, Sison's unspeakable brutalization) by evoking a hidden significance prefigured in it, an evocation both retrospective and anticipatory in effect and in so doing memorializing an eroticized, Orphic harmony of nature and man (note the recurrent image of rain, wind, tropes of the spirit) and summoning in vision the lineaments of a long expected reunion many times postponed, a communal celebration suggested in microcosm by Sison's communication to his children: "Across Blue Waters" [130] and "To Jasm, My Captive Child" [134]. This prophetic impulse both preserves the anguish of a repressive order (class domination, fascist instrumentalization of life) and supersedes it. in much the same way as the Promethean refusal of taboos and prohibitions – its text of negations and annulments – contains within it an affirmation of a liberated realm of gratified desire. This impulse we encounter everyday as an inherent quality of the labor process itself whose end, for humans, is already anticipated in thought, consciousness, above all in the imagination.

Intrinsically dialectical in operation and materialist in grounding, this prophetic/utopian tendency in Sison's poems – a trait one discovers as an obsessive rhythm in *Florante at Laura,* Rizal's novels, Bulosan's and Amado Hernandez's writings– explains the choice of allegory as a formal device to transmute the individualized flux of experience into the differential system of rhetorical figuration. This allegorical drive manifests itself most vividly in "Against the Monster on the Land" [36]. "The Woman and the Strange Eagle" [32] and "Defy the Reptile" [42] which, rehearsing a historical moment of demystification converts the narrative sequence into the illusion-breaking stasis of parable.

What happens in allegory is this: instead of inducing an easy reconciliation of antinomies, an existential leap into faith where all class antagonisms vanish and rebellious desire is pacified, allegory heightens the tension between signifier and signified, between object and subject, thereby foiling empathy and establishing the temporary distance required for generating critical judgment and ultimately cathartic action. Nowhere is this allegorical method of structuring more intensely sustained than in "Fragments of a Nightmare" [68], Sison's "inferno" stage to a quite undivine comedy.

It is obvious that a reading of "Fragments" will not add to one's conceptual understanding of Sison's suffering and the issues at stake. Such an effort can be advanced by grasping the evidence and import of all his published testimonies. What this mode of oblique staging unfolds is precisely the primordial incongruity between what exists and what can be, the disparity between fact and possibility, the inassimilable dissonance between the reality principle and the pleasure principle which may be how Sison aims to register the fact of repression, the dominance of commodity-fetishism, in our neocolonized society with its host of internal contradictions.

Allegory then, as process of mediating opposites, focuses on the crux of the contradictions and discharges a call, a polemical challenge. It images the transitional movement of difference from passive contemplation to active involvement, converting objects into process, the process of social production and of social relations. Note the fusion of perceived and perceiver. "As I struggle and scream for air, / American rock music screens my screams / Outside the torture chamber" [80].

Sison compels us to accompany him in his abortive Virgilian pilgrimage. For in this ironic, inverted realm of the antiromance, the legendary paradise longed for, the classless society which is the object of humanity's quest, is displaced by a double estrangement: imprisonment as fact and as metaphor. Hinted in Hemandez' lines quoted here as epigraph, the duplicity of imprisonment reveals itself as a temporary unity of opposites, a momentary paralysis but also a phase of becoming. By employing the imperative and subjunctive mood, a dialogic and carnivalisque technique (Bakhtin), Sison seeks to preempt any idea of organic plenitude or mimetic equivalence between language and reality which would thereby make art a self-sufficient, autotelic object, the hypostasis of psychic drives in some Lacanian prison of the Imaginary.

What Sison's poems consistently undermine is the aura of a language of self-presence (whose libidinal investment one finds in the exuberance of Villa or Joaquin), a language of ritualized sublimation which is incessantly decentered by the heterogeneity of imagery and tone in "Fragments." The logic of this somewhat convulsed style and the theoretical rationale for revolutionary art in general (Sison's included) are succinctly expressed by Walter Benjamin and Christopher Caudwell:

> The utilization of dream-elements in waking is the textbook example of dialectical thought. Hence dialectical thought is the organ of historical awakening. Every epoch not only dreams the next, but while dreaming impels it towards wakefulness. It bears its end within itself, and reveals it – as Hegel already recognized – by a ruse. With the upheaval of the market economy, we begin to recognize the monuments of the bourgeoisie as ruins even before they have crumbled. –Benjamin, "Paris, Capital of the 19th Century"

> Of the future one can only dream – with greater or less success. Even dream is determined, and a movement in dream reflects perhaps a real movement into daylight of material phenomena at present unrecognized. That is why it is possible to dream with accuracy of the future – in other words, to predict scientifically. This is the prophetic and world-creating power of dream. It derives its world-creating power, not by virtue of being dream… but because it reflects in the sphere of thought a movement which, with the help of dream, can be fully realized in practice. It draws its creative power, like the poetry of the harvest festival, from its value as a guide and spur to action, It is dream already passed out of the sphere of dream into that of social revolution. It is the dream, not of an individual, but of a man reflecting in his individual consciousness the creative role of a whole class, whose movement is given in the material conditions of society. – Caudwell, *Illusion and Reality*.

Long before I encountered the Index editor in London last year, my intervention in the cultural front took the form of a booklet *The Radical Tradition in Philippine Literature* (1971) where I pointed out in one chapter how Sison's 1961 collection *Brothers* succeeded "in projecting the democratic tendencies of the Filipino bourgeoisie" in the period of Recto's nationalist crusade. Subsequently, a qualitative leap 'occurred in the mid-1960s. In hindsight, I should now qualify that it is rather the progressive national-democratic ideology of our intelligentsia aligned with class-conscious workers and peasants that constitute the enabling condition of possibility for Brothers. For this volume, such conditions – a description of which, for the Marxist critic, replaces any mere formalist explication of texts – are the intensifying class confrontations in city and countryside to which we are all witnesses in which the whole society (as the political prisoners testify in Pintig and Pumipiglas) is unveiled as a huge, tumultuous prison replicating the State institution and thus allowing the victims to recuperate in the same breath their oneness and integrity with those who are poised to blast their chains and bars in one last decisive, apocalyptic act of liberation.

Let us then celebrate its foreshadowed advent with the voice of our comrade Sison who, from the depths of the military dungeon, inspires us with his unrelentingly lucid courage and selflessly redeeming hope.

– E. San Juan, Jr.

## Beyond Autobiography

Reading through the poems in *Prison and Beyond,* one is apt to get habituated to the stark diction and militant tone of the prison poems, only to be jarred by the "poetic" manner of the pieces written between 1958 and 1961. Jose Ma. Sison's first book of poems was published in 1962. Brothers introduced readers in the young poet's time to poems which, in the late years of the 1950s, dared to be (against the fashion of the times) political poetry. The poems were an attempt to break away from the aestheticist concerns of his contemporaries, but the poet had found it difficult at that stage to forge a style demanded by his subject matter and intentions. There simply were no models in the local tradition of Philippine writing in English he could go back to, except such discredited or unfashionable poets like R. Zulueta da Costa ("Like the Molave"), Aurelio Alvero ("1896"), or, at best, the expatriate Carlos Bulosan ("If You Want to Know What We Are").

In the waning years of the Cold War decade, Sison was courting critical doom by defying the reigning formalist dicta against "propaganda" in poetry. But the social realities in the poet's young manhood at the University of the Philippines could not be glossed over by the verbal witchery that elder poets and his peers cultivated in their verses. Glimpses of unjust structures, brutishness, corruption and callousness together presented a bleak landscape that the young poet hoped could be set aright. "Carnival" gave a tawdry microcosm of Philippine society as peopled by "bribeable bureaucrats," "politicians and professional specialists," pedants, poets and "charity ladies." In "These Scavengers," children digging for food at garbage heaps occasioned an indictment of the hollowness of religious platitudes when not translated into deeds. Petit-bourgeois rebels who were too easily seduced by wealth and power inspired the poet with contempt, and he pictured them as "trophies" to be displayed in the clubs of the rich and the powerful in "The Fish Stuffed." And "The Massacre," a poem commemorating the notorious Maliwalu massacre, sounded a call to vengeance that would bring to justice the perpetrators of a heinous crime against peasants.

Although Sison's subject matter and intentions in the above poems were a repudiation of much of the poetry his contemporaries were writing, he found himself caught up in the same intoxication with modernist poetry found among post-war exponents of elliptical syntax and highly personal, almost idiosyncratic diction, like Amado Unite, Oscar de Zuniga and Alejandrino G. Hufana. Those were literary times when existentialism was in flower and our writers in English, in a period of political reaction steered clear of what were thought to be "vulgarities" of social reality, and concentrated instead on the articulation of despair in a society where human venalities were more comfortably explained away as inevitable ills in an absurd universe. As though to prove that his political views and insights were as valid material for poetry as anguish and loneliness, Sison adopted the "modernist" manner of the reigning models from Western poetry and of his contemporaries at UP. The option had the effect of making his poems, as political utterance, accessible mainly to the elite circle of writers, teachers and students of literature in the Academe. Unfortunately, that audience had been tamed by Cold War propaganda emanating from the USIS into suspecting any contemporary literary work by a Filipino that smelled vaguely of "ideas" or, worse yet, "ideology." In such a setting, Sison's art was boxed in by the paradox of affecting the manner of "artistic" contemporaries even as he revolted against the intellectual vacuousness of their poetic output.

In 1971, Sison repudiated, "with the exception of five or six," his poems in Brothers. The occasion was the first national congress of PAKSA, a progressive writers organization. In a message, he made an act of self-criticism, saying that "the bulk of the poems, cannot pass the test of proletarian revolutionary criticism." He expressed the hope that "with this repudiation I shall be able to write better poems."

As early as 1968, Sison was on the way to writing what he regarded as "better" poems. "The Guerrilla Is Like a Poet" [24] was unlike his earlier poems – Sison had purged his lines of their former load of self-conscious imagery compounded of modifiers and syntactical constructions that all but choked out detail. The resulting transparency and impact of the poet's language was a relief from the intellectual coyness of the "arty" output of many of his contemporaries. The poem marked the beginning of Sison's break-away from the tradition of English writing to which his training as an English major had pegged his poetry.

*Prison and Beyond* shows Sison the poet crossing over to another tradition of writing in the Philippines, his theoretical and practical work in the national democratic movement having led him to the key question of committed writing in the beginning of the 1970s. "For whom?" The question was originally posed by Mao Zedong in the context of writing for the Chinese Revolution when this was still seven years away from final victory. In the writing scene in the Philippines, Mao's question had cut through so much critical underbrush, opening up a path for young writers seeking participation in the struggle for social change. It became clear to these writers that it was their intended audience that would set the conditions for a meaningful encounter between text and reader. Their intended audience was the Filipino masses, and the masses could be reached only through any one of the vernacular languages. Some of those writing in English but could afford to choose, opted for Pilipino. Others who could not, faced the prospect of ceasing to write altogether.

But giving up writing was not the sole option available to nationalist poets and fictionists who could not handle Pilipino as a literary medium. Sison's example showed them the radical way. Indeed, English was a language that allowed the Filipino writer to reach only an elite readership. That readership, however, could be broadened provided one was willing to write against the grain of established tradition in pursuit of a higher, social good. Sison, as the poems written since "The Guerrilla Is Like a Poet," would attest, has cut out from his verse characteristics highly-prized by the critical orthodoxy in contemporary writing in English, such as "ambiguity," "paradox," "wit," etc. The pruning job has resulted often in the lucidity of direct speech which, theoretically at least, makes his poems accessible to a wider audience who could read in English, but lacks the specialized literary training that is a requisite for the appreciation of much of Filipino poetry in English.

The long poem "Fragments of a Nightmare" [68] clarifies the contribution of Sison's example in *Prison and Beyond* to what, for want of a better term, might be called the "indigenization" of Philippine writing in English. The poem stands as the centerpiece of Sison's second book, a chronicle of the poet's arrest, interrogation, torture and detention that lacerates the imagination as no previous Filipino work of art has ever done. The hellish experience has been cast, in the form of an allegory about a man who has had to wrestle with demons, emerging from the test stronger, more resolute and indomitable. The result is a work unparallelled in the entire history of Philippine literature as a poetic rendering of a systematic and ruthless process of breaking a man down through extreme mental and physical torment.

A reading of "Fragments of a Nightmare" sears into the consciousness questions on human endurance. How much pain can the flesh absorb? How much anxiety can the spirit weather? What activates a victim's inner reserves and gives him power to prevail over his tormentors? Without the help of grand rhetorical artifices, the poem succeeds in galvanizing us against torture as a dastardly method of making a man betray his comrades and cause. The reader is aware that the speaking voice is that of Jose Ma. Sison, but he is confronted with self-denying understatement made possible by the use of a low-keyed allegory about a man who had had to wrestle with demons and survived without surrendering his faith. Ultimately, the poem goes beyond autobiography. By the force of Sison's allegorical method, the extreme test that the prisoner undergoes becomes the testing of every political prisoner who endures and survives because he has been buoyed up by solidarity with all men in struggle against injustice and repression.

In *Prison and Beyond,* Sison has chosen to be evaluated outside of the tradition from which he got his start as a poet. In crossing over to another tradition, the poet has chosen to be judged alongside Jose Rizal ("Mi Ultimo Adios"), Aurelio Tolentino ("Kahapon, Ngayon at Bukas," the poem), Jose Corazon de Jesus ("Sa Dakong Silangan") and Amado V. Hernandez ("Bayang Malaya"). In that company, Jose Ma. Sison is assured of a place of honor.

– Bienvenido Lumbera

## Politics and Faith

*His political faith.*
*The years of struggle demanded of him by that faith.*
*The years in prison demanded from him by his detractors*
*as a result of that struggle.*

These are what form and frame the metaphors and the images that stud the poetry of Jose Maria Sison. In this wise is this poet essentially honest for when we sum it up, this is the triad that makes up his life.

I am tempted to refer to his being instead, but I am held back by a niggling doubt – as to whether or not his politics allows him a metaphysics. Those who do allow it in their lives, however, should not be faulted if they see vegetations of it in his poems. That may be why some of us tend to conjure his politics as a kind of faith, giving to it even, some kind of a religious dimension.

Heresy that may be to some, but how best describe the honesty of his humanity?

For a deep sense of humanity it is that informs each and every poem in this collection, a deep and personal and even (again heresy this) mystical humanity. Surprising that may be to some also, particularly those more familiar with his prose (militant, methodical and to others maniacal) and more so with the prose written about him (in the main damning and derogatory). A prose of extremes then is what we've had mainly of this man and on him – but that's to be expected for controversy is, but certainly, almost of the essence of his life and work.

But detract from the prose we may, for here Jose Maria Sison is a poet.

This isn't saying, though, that he's any different as a result or that what he has here is a different face. The full integration of life and work (and one must count here his creative work as well) remains.

Only the telling of it, or the saying of it, is different – for poetry is, most assuredly, different from prose.

And different not only in the manner of it but even, in a way, in the sense of it – for though one may quibble with the motivation and the underlying honesty of prose because direct and to the point, one may not do so with poetry.

Poetry assumes a different dimension in that it is another way of telling or speaking the truth. And while truth is pure and indivisible, the telling of it and the speaking of it comes differently with prose as it does with poetry.

Poetry is the crystallization of it and therefore hardly utilitarian.

Therefore we say: if Jose Maria Sison lives simply for his politics he could very well have been satisfied, he could very well have been content, to limit himself to prose.

But there is an honesty to this man as I said and that is the honesty of his humanity as unveiled through these poems (we use veil here to underscore this aspect of him that has been shrouded over). Moreover, it is an honesty that should be acknowledged, whether willingly or grudgingly, precisely because it is human and acknowledgment of the human in others increases our own humanity.

Therefore, because human, there is love here as much as there is anger, for these are our most elemental (though hardly elementary) passions.

Again not elementary, they talk about friends and enemies – the metaphors of them and the images of them carrying in power and intensity, in reach and in grasp, as the nearness of them to the poet and the distance between them and the poet change. Still, whether close or whether distanced, they are never abstract.

This is so because all is real to the poet.

His wife is real:
> *In the old poem of our youth eighteen years ago*
> *We walked hand in hand through the Diliman cogon.*
> *We've gone a long way from then and there;*
> *Not only cold nights have we braved but storms.*

His children are real:
> *Across blue waters*
> *We smile to each other.*
> *For us to embrace and kiss*
> *We dispatch the waves.* [130]

His friends are as real as brothers:
> *Among green leaves my brother fell on soil.*
> *On his forehead was his faith marked red*

> *By a bullet above sight, reaching brain,*
> *Bringing blood below to his mouth agape*
> *Kissed at last by the bride of hunger fond of delay.*

His enemies are real in their peculiarity:
> *Cast away he who talks of himself*
> *Across the table*
> *While men die in battlefields*
> *For those who have long endured*
> *In silence and who have found their voice*
> *Deafeningly sure*
> *While all along the coffeehouse charlatan*
> *Loudly essays his opportune grace*
> *In every period*
> *Within his crammy precinct.*

Prison is real:
> *They call the prisoner an ant*
> *They can fool and play with*
> *No matter how tight the cell*
> *It is an arena of struggle*
>
> *The heroic prisoner is like a giant:*
> *He draws his strength from the masses,*
> *His spirit is like a bird looking down:*
> *Oh. how small are all the monsters below!* [106]

And, too, his own freedom:
> *A spirit as active and free as mine*

> *Can never be entombed in a cell.*
> *I shall continue to rise*
> *In defiance of the somnolent bell.* [120]

All, indeed, is real to the poet.
> And all is real to this poet. As it should be.

> – Alfredo Navarro Salanga

## From Literature to Revolution

As this is being written, confrontations between the students and the military continue in the streets of Manila. Meetings among professionals and workers are conducted in closed halls, while the reigning dictatorship, in an effort to divide the ranks of the opposition, issues warnings against "radicals" and "subversives." The nation is going through a revolutionary situation, with the New People's Army, the military arm of the Communist Party of the Philippines, intensifying guerrilla war in the countryside, raiding military outposts, and expanding its membership. Six years ago, Jose Maria Sison was arrested by the military on charges of being the Chairman of the Communist Party of the Philippines. Today, Sison is in solitary confinement at a military stockade. If the military is to be believed, Sison continues to influence events in absentia.

Perhaps no contemporary writer has been credited by the State itself to have exerted such a pervasive influence on thought and national events. The last time a similar phenomenon occurred was in the 19th century, in the instance of Jose Rizal. Claro Recto, who worked within the canons of the 19th century intellectuals, never succeeded in achieving such an immediately large influence.

Coming after Recto, Sison continues within the 19th century intellectual tradition. The essential aspect of this tradition measures a writer's stature not so much by the volume of his works as by his capacity to assume public responsibility. The writer's concern for literature, for art and aesthetic, becomes continuous with his concern to recreate society, to establish institutions, and to elevate the quality of life of a people. The aesthetic concern finds its issues not only in art but in revolutionizing culture and society.

Such are the concerns that underlie Sison's writings. Strangely, it was this concern that seemed to have alienated him from the literary mainstream of the 1950s.

In the 1950s, the quality of arts and letters reflected the fears and vacillations generated by the McCarthyist witchhunt and the policy of containment of the United States. The investigations of writers and academicians by Congress in the United States promoted either a chauvinistic or an apolitical Liberalism. Writers who formerly flirted with Marxist ideas either took a firmly nationalist anti-Communist stance, or wrote those "confessions" which purported to expose the devastating effect of ideology on art. The examples of George Orwell, Stephen Spender, Andre Gide, and lgnazio Silone were held up by the promoters of apolitical liberalism as the testimony of the subtly dire effects of ideology on the creativity and freedom of the artist.

This was the climate which we imbibed in the 1950s, when academicians and intellectuals were being hounded by the Committee on Un-Filipino Activities, (CUFA), later the Committee on Anti-Filipino Activities, (CAFA). Even the reading of Rizal's writings became the subject of a long congressional debate. In place of politically committed literature, the cultural scene was deluged with abstract modernist art, the writings of

Freud, Jung, and Kierkegaard; and the novels of Hemingway, Fitzgerald, Faulkner and Henry Miller.

It was at this time that I came to know Jose Ma. Sison. He had acted in bit parts in some theatre productions of Wilfredo Ma. Guerrero in his undergraduate years. One summer, after he had finished his AB in English, cum laude, he came to see me at the dorm with the manuscript of a novel.

Although at the time we prided ourselves in being alive to the issues of the day – that period being the intensification of the McCarthyist witchhunt, resulting in the suspension of the writ of habeas corpus – Sison's novel somehow failed to elicit from us an immediate response. The novel had something to do with the agrarian problem in Luzon, involving sugarcane workers. The central character, confronted with the fact of a decaying feudalism, was too involved in specific social and historical details – scenes and incidents of an agrarian community which was beyond our ken of appreciation.

That was the first time I had met Sison. The CAFA witchhunt had absorbed our attention, but, looking back, we had reacted to it in a very abstract way. We had regarded the McCarthyist investigations – with their manufacture of evidence; their irresponsible smear campaign against dissenters and their blacklist of nonconformists – we had regarded all this as either a form of political perversion or a simple case of stupidity. We therefore were not inclined to take the congressional investigations seriously – confident that we could hold on to our "civilized values" against the obviously backward and Philistine impulses of some illiterate sectors of society.

We were too naive. It took us a decade to realize that the politics of McCarthyism was a mask, that it concealed the concrete reality of a repression being systematically unleashed against farmers and workers who were fighting for a decent form of survival. The facts and the concrete details became real to us later. But in the 1950s in Manila, and particularly in the academe, we reacted to the congressional investigations in a very abstract way, on the level of political principles. Hence our writings failed to come to grips with the social reality that underlie what seemed merely to be the personal aberration of some laymen and politicians. It would appear that Sison – who comes from Ilocos – had grasped the truth of the situation and, in his novel, made an effort to put political principles in their social and historical context the way Marx perceived historical materialism within the Hegelian dialectics. But it was because of his too concrete a sense of the political problems, at the time that I failed to respond to his novel. There was none in it of the threatened emasculation of a Jake Barnes or the sense of lostness of Jay Gatsby.

We conducted discussions and symposia on freedom and civil liberties, but our interest in freedom was precisely ineffectual because it was rooted in our nonconformism rather than in concrete social and political interests.

The same apolitical sense made me miss the very compelling quality of the poems in *Brothers* when I wrote the introduction to the book in 1960.

It would appear that in the writing of the poems in *Brothers*, Sison was employing a revolutionary aesthetics. The poems are inspired, not by the conventions of literature, but by the need to relate to facts in Philippine social life. Contrary to the formal conventions of the decade, Sison at times would invent no metaphor but speak directly.

*In that central part of the country the helpless corpse*
*Received rifle butts on the stomach pit.*

The lines themselves behave as correlate objects, functioning both as medium and message simultaneously. They behave as significations, not of ideas, but of social actuality.

No book of poems written or published during this period achieved a similar documentation of the reality that was the root of the social and political unrest that confronted our generation. The ensuing issues were to be analyzed more deeply in the next decades, and Sison himself participated in a central way in the analysis and clarification of those political and social questions.

But even as early as the late 1950s, he seems to have grasped the roots of our political problems.

*Brothers*, then, is significant in its comprehensive statement of what was later to be Sison's preoccupation, namely, to present the contradictions in the national reality concretely, to identify the various components of the contradictions, and to uphold revolution as the logical resolution of the national problem. It is possible to say that the poems in Brothers serve as preparatory statements of Sison's revolutionary articulation on the Philippine situation. "The Imperial Game" (1960), "Last Sunday" (1958), "Carnival" (1959), "Across the Sun Drenched Square" (1958) anticipated the national perception of Philippine social problems to which the Filipino writer would respond only in the late 1960s and Seventies, while "One Nazarite Rebel" shows the direction through which liberation from the prevailing social condition could be achieved.

What is significant about "One Nazarite Rebel" is that in 1959 the idea of the oppressed being able to break the bonds of their oppression was not in the public mind. The Communist Party of the Philippines, under the leadership of the Lavas, had been decimated; by the 1960s it was considered a "nuisance" or merely a convenient reference to increase the military budget. The legal opposition among the political parties, on the other hand, could not assume the role of national leadership. The Nationalista and the Liberal Party reflected more the constant maneuvers of the oligarchs to capture temporary political power in order to advance the economic interests of the sector which they represented or which financed their political campaigns. Rebellion or revolution, in its positive liberating function, was not in the popular imagination.

In 1967, Sison published a collection of essays entitled, *Struggle for National Democracy*. The book collates a number of speeches delivered on various occasions dealing with specific issues and problems of Philippine society. The essays may be considered as rendering in prose and in analytical terms the essential problems that the poems in *Brothers* deal with. With *Struggle for National Democracy* Sison had eventually identified three main sources of the national problem: (1) American imperialism; (2) the semi-feudal economy and social relations prevailing in the country; and (3) the role of the bureaucrat in both abetting and compounding the problems.

In 1971, a book entitled *Philippine Society and Revolution* (PSR) by one Amado Guerrero was published. The military claims that "Amado Guerrero" was the pseudonym of Jose Ma. Sison. If this is true, then Sison in 1970, was the most influential Filipino writer after Rizal.

PSR was immediately translated into Tagalog and into several languages. Pirated editions were distributed abroad. In Manila, the book immediately enjoyed a brisk sale and until the declaration of martial law, when it became dangerous to be found possessing a copy of it, PSR was virtually the Red Book among the youth.

I do not want to exaggerate. PSR did not create the First Quarter Storm. It did not inspire the upsurge of protest and mass action that Marcos called "the national state of rebellion" which he said compelled him to declare martial law. The economic and social conditions of the country were at the root of the organized protests in the first years of the seventies, and when PSR appeared on the scene, the First Quarter Storm had already, so to speak, erupted. But PSR contributed so much to the analysis of contemporary Philippine problems. Academics reacted to what they called "over-simplifications" in the analysis of Philippine problems in PSR. If PSR reduced Philippine problems into simple terms, it also allowed what indeed was a complex situation to be comprehended.

The colonial question in the Philippines had indeed spawned a school of confusion. It had diversified into a complex of specific issues, so overwhelming in their cumulative impact that the Filipino people, as a whole, could only react to the petty details that directly affected them.

Recto exposed the situation of continued dependence of the country after it was supposed to have acquired its independence, but concentrated his analysis on the issue of international relations and foreign policy. The intelligentsia, on the other hand, concerned itself with the cultural superstructure, depicting the effects of colonialism on Filipino attitudes, habits, and memories. Public opinion, acting on what was obvious and directly touching individual lives, alternately attacked graft and corruption in government; bad roads; uncollected garbage; police abuses; the rise of criminality, etc.

It is this quality of thought, this obsession with revolution if you will, that constitutes the unity of these poems. This quality informs the poems written as early as the late 1950s and those composed inside Sison's detention cell.

Sometime in the late 1960s, in a message to PAKSA, Sison disavowed some of his earlier poetic productions. He said some of the poems in *Brothers* relate to different period and, therefore, may be wanting in political and revolutionary relevance. I find this judgement unsatisfactory. All the poems in these volume show us the way of welding the creative process to revolutionary practice, of fulfilling the demands of art and the requirements of politics.

The proper relationship between literature and politics has always been a problematic one in our times, although it was never so for those writers who had openly used social and political issues as central subject of their writings or to whom the political question was an overriding concern in their literary aesthetics. Certainly, the question was not a problematic one for Dante in the writing of the *Divine Comedy* or, in the modern period, for such writers as Wordsworth, Byron and, in the contemporary period, for Silone, Sartre or Malraux. Nonetheless, it has become a crucial problem for contemporary literature.

The divide between art and political concern was part of the main point of the American Formalists – the very liberal group that, frightened by McCarthyism, sought to discredit socialist writing as a category of literature.

In the Philippines, the issue of politics and art has been debated since those scoundrel times of CAFA days and has even more been intensely discussed since the upsurge of the First Quarter Storm. It was reflective of the vacillations of some writers that, after martial law, the debate appeared to have been resolved by them in favor of an effete aesthetics. It was part of their pretense to say that their partial engagement with politics had inevitably led them to the conclusion that a writer must serve the claims of literary aesthetics alone. The avowals of those writers cease to be convincing when considered against the haste with which they sought to finish their manuscript for the deadlines of contests sponsored by the fascist regime. It is possible to say that PSR lent the popular anger during the First Quarter Storm a sense of direction. It invited us to review the history of the country and the course which Philippine society had taken as a result of the history of colonialism.

No single book in the Post-War era had exposed more fully the nature of Philippine feudal conditions, the reinforcement it received from imperialist interest and how the conditions generated by feudalism and imperialism found issue in our behavior, attitudes, morals, and manners. No other book, to my knowledge, provides us the key to the understanding of Philippine society.

It was this simple exposition of Philippine reality, with its explicit faith in the capability of the people to change the course of history and, by implication, their individual destinies, that made PSR the guiding spirit of the First Quarter Storm and, if the military is to be believed, of the revolutionary movement as a whole.

In reading the poetry of Jose Maria Sison, then, we must go beyond their literary qualities. This is not to say that they are remiss in literary values. Rather, the literary significance of these poems derive from the unique quality of thought or consciousness that informs each poem or which organizes each of them. Most poems written in prison seldom go beyond being a personal testimony of the author. This is so of Balagtas' "Kay Selya" or of Rizal's "Mi Ultimo Adios". The poems written in prison in this volume contain some elements of personal testimony, of course. But even in the more confessional poems, where the author relates in seemingly veiled terms (through the metaphor of a nightmare) his incarceration, the sense of terror is detached from self. The recital of the horror of torture becomes a form of affirming the capacity of man in withstanding torture and humiliation in favor of comrades and principles and the revolution.

A critic once observed that the poetry of Teresa of Avila is suffused with God. In an analogous way, the poetry of Sison is suffused with the idea of revolution. Even the purely descriptive poems, or those which appear to be simply exercises in wit and metaphor, nature or objects or situations inevitably relate themselves to certain aspects of the revolutionary struggle. In that now famous single piece, "The Guerilla Is Like a Poet" [68] even the techniques and tactics of the creative process is turned into possibilities and postures of revolutionary armed struggle.

The courage of Jose Maria Sison in standing for a revolutionary aesthetics even behind the walls of his solitary confinement and, seemingly, against the sanctions of prevailing aesthetic tastes forms part of my continuing admiration for him. He, together with such contemporaries as E. San Juan, Emmanuel Lacaba, Edel Garcellano, and Gelacio Guillermo have persevered on the idea that it takes courage to live the literary life as it does to make a stand on political questions. It takes integrity to become a writer.

– Petronilo Bn. Daroy

## The Legacy of Mao and Sison in People's Literature

The literary legacy of Chairman Mao Zedong is pervasive in the national democratic movement led by its premier writer and theoretician Jose Maria Sison.

The people's literature, bearing the legacy of both poets and revolutionaries and reflecting the struggles of workers, peasants, urban poor, students, teachers, women, religious, and other marginalized sectors in Philippine society, was summed up after 25 years in several symposia, books, and articles.

The founders and heirs of the *Panitikan para sa Kaunlaran ng Sambayanan* (PAKSA), writers, founded in 1971 on the basis of the aesthetics assimilated from Mao's *Talks at the Yenan Forum on Art and Literature,* published *Rebolusyonaryong Panunuring Masa sa Sining at Panitikan* (Revolutionary Mass Criticism in Art and Literature), containing the original documents of PAKSA's founding congress on the genres of drama, short story, song, and poetry, a message from Jose Maria Sison; his article "Tasks of Cadres in Cultural Work"; Mao's Talks at the Yenan Forum; and Lu Xun's "Thoughts on the League of Left Writers."

Also included are the documents on visual arts prepared by the Nagkakaisang Progresibong Artista at Arkitekto or NPAA (Alliance of Progressive Artists and Architects), also inspired by Mao's aesthetics, assessing the uses of the poster, illustration and editorial cartoon, comics, painting, photography, and folk art in popularizing national democratic ideas. PAKSA and NPAA were among the groups formed after the First Quarter Storm of 1970.

With the declaration of martial law in 1972, President Ferdinand Marcos unleashed a military campaign against the fast-developing national democratic movement which had already opened several guerrilla fronts. PAKSA, along with all national democratic organizations, went underground, producing literary works tailored to the requirements of war in the countryside. In the cities, where censorship was strictly enforced, cadres put out underground publications.

Many writers were drawn to the struggle against the dictatorship. They read up on Marxism–Leninism–Mao Zedong Thought, Jose Maria Sison's *Struggle for National Democracy*, Amado Guerrero's *Philippine Society and Revolution*, and also Frantz Fanon's The Wretched of the Earth, Paolo Freire's *Pedagogy of the Oppressed*, and other Third World writers. Besides the nationalist writings of Teodoro Agoncillo, Amado V. Hernandez, and Renato Constantino, they also studied the works of Bertolt Brecht, George Lukacs, and later Antonio Gramsci and Louis Althusser. The writings of those drawn to the national democratic struggle thus took on a broad counter-hegemonic perspective.

The impetus for these progressive literary efforts in the 1970s was provided by the national democratic writers and cadres. With the imposition of martial law, the liberals and social democrats within the broad anti-Marcos movement began to realize the meaning of the national democratic struggle against US imperialism, feudalism, and bureaucrat-capitalism.

Given the censorship in the cities, they had to resort to what was called the "literature of circumvention" or "the literature of detour" – using cunning and subterfuge through literary devices such as allegory – in exposing or attacking the enemy in State-controlled publications. A number of city-bred writers and intellectuals helped train cadres in literary and cultural production.

In the countryside where guerrilla fronts had begun to develop and expand, cadres put out periodicals for specific revolutionary purposes and for specific audiences. They followed the guidelines in Talks at the Yenan Forum.

Underground literature is assessed in *The Literature of National Democracy* (1992) by Gelacio Guillermo and *The New Mass Art and Literature* (1988) by Kris Montanez. National democratic literature as well as counter-hegemonic writings in general have been studied by critics such as Bienvenido Lumbera (*Revaluation,* 1984), Nicanor Tiongson et al. (*Politics of Culture,* 1984), Epifanio San Juan Jr. (*Towards a People's Literature,* 1984; *Only in Struggle,* 1989), Elmer A, Ordonez (*The Other View: Philippine Writing and Culture,* 1989), Alice Guillermo (*The Covert Presence and Other Essays on Politics and Culture,* 1989), and Edel Garcellano (*Intertext,* 1990).

Monico Atienza's *Kilusang Pambansang Demokratiko sa Wika* (The National Democratic Movement on Language, 1992) documents the steps taken by the movement to enhance and propagate Filipino. Many writers in English drawn to the movement have since turned to using Filipino as their literary vehicle.

With the advent in the 1980s of post-structuralism, particularly the critical methods of Marxist and feminist deconstruction, a new generation of progressive critics has helped in the academic but important task of opening up the literary canon (long the preserve of formalist critics) and introducing national democratic, emergent, or counter-hegemonic literatures in school curriculums, book stores, and libraries. The general guidelines of the *Talks at the Yenan Forum* are now incorporated in the National Democratic program on the development of a nationalist, scientific and mass-based culture.

Mao's writings on art, literature and culture as well as Lu Xun's works reached the Philippines in the 60s, with Jose Maria Sison, chairman of the Kabataang Makabayan, giving lectures seeking to initiate a cultural revolution in the manner of China's May Fourth Movement. Specifically Sison called for a Second Propaganda Movement (the first was conducted by *ilustrados* like Jose Rizal and Marcelo del Pilar a decade before the outbreak of the 1896 Philippine Revolution) at a time when the old Communist Party became moribund. His lecture is included in the *Struggle for National Democracy,* a theoretical application of Marxism–Leninism–Mao Zedong Thought and required reading for youth activists.

In the late 60s young writers inspired by the poetry of Sison (e.g. "The Guerrilla is Like a Poet") and Hernandez's novel *Mga Ibong Mandaragit* and his prison poems (e.g. "Isang Dipang Langit") turned away from bourgeois literary concerns and began writing protest and eventually, national democratic literature in the genres of poetry, fiction, drama, and popular and folk forms to popularize the struggle. In 1970, in the midst of the massive demonstrations of the First Quarter Storm, these writers became the founders of PAKSA.

The writers declared that literature should serve the masses and be written in the national language. Their first demonstration on 2 April 1971 called for "Literature for a National Cultural Revolution." Their manifesto made clear that the writers had the duty of producing literature that is involved in realizing the aspirations of the oppressed people, a literature directed at the rottenness of society, a literature for the masses that would constitute a formidable revolutionary force to crush American imperialist exploiters – towards national democracy.

In his message to the founding congress of PAKSA on 18–19 December 1971, Sison reiterated the relevance of *Talks at the Yenan Forum*. He enjoined the members to strengthen their revolutionary class stand, practice criticism and self- criticism, and infuse revolutionary class content into the different literary forms.

Since then, the movement's cultural workers have produced a solid body of works that acquired not only bulk but a cogency that helped the people in the struggle against the dictatorial regime, leading to Marcos' downfall in the people power uprising in EDSA in 1986. However, the repressive and ideological State apparatuses remained intact, making possible the transfer of political and economic control to another set of oligarchs headed by Corazon Aquino who kept a veneer of liberal democracy.

Cultural workers were kept busy, many of them surfacing in the cities where they set up publications, put on plays, and held exhibits. Protest literature during the martial law period were published in three volumes of *Kamao* put out by the Cultural Center of the Philippines, once the venue of the Marcos elite and now relatively open to the masses.

Works during martial law have appeared in underground periodicals including *Liberation, Ulos, Kamao,* and *Taliba ng Bayan*. They have been compiled and edited resulting in a number of underground books such as *Tula ng Rebolusyong Filipino* (1982) 1982 and *Magsasaka: Ang Bayaning Di Kilala* (1984), as well as aboveground publications such as *New Philippine Writing* (1983), *Politics and Culture* (1985), *Versus* (1986), *Kamao* (1987), STR (1989), and books published abroad such as *Pintig* (Hongkong,1979) and *The Guerrilla Is Like a Poet* (Canada, 1989). Also published were individual author titles such as the novel *Hulagpos (Break Away)* (1981) by Mano de Verdades Posadas, *Prison Poems and Beyond* (1984) by Jose Maria Sison, poetry collection *Why Caged Pigeons?* (1985) by Mila Aguilar, *Alab* (1984), poetry collection *Moon's Face* (1989) by Alan Jazmines, the novel *Gera* (1991) by Ruth Firmeza, *Sa Tungki ng Ilong ng Kaaway: Talambuhay ni Tatang* (Under the Enemy's Nose: The Autobiography of Tatang, 1988), the novel *Sebyo* (1989) by Carlos Humberto, *The New Mass Art and Literature* (1988) and *Poems* (1989) by Kriz Montanez, and *Ang Panitikan ng Pambansang Demokrasya* (Literature of the National Democratic Movement, 1990) by Gelacio Guillermo.

Guillermo sums up the literature of national democracy in several essays, including one on post-EDSA literature, another on revolutionary peasant literature, and others on developing new writers from the masses, translation work for the masses, national, scientific, and mass-based culture, and the poetry of Sison as a "people's statesman." The article "Revolutionary Peasant Literature" is a creative application of the basic principles of Mao's literary theory as well as the tenets of people's war in Philippine Society and Revolution and Specific Characteristics of People's War by Amado Guerrero (nom de plume of Jose Maria Sison).

Guillermo outlines the principles as follows: the guiding role of proletarian ideology in the production of peasant literature; literature advancing the struggle for national democracy, the main content of which is peasant emancipation from feudal and semifeudal bondage; development of literature on the principle of "from the masses, to the masses," which involves popularization and raising of standards; literary production, dissemination, and improvement as a mass undertaking; and the production and dissemination of peasant literature.

Guillermo envisages the countryside as the political, economic, military, and cultural bastion of the revolution in order to "defend people's gains and to advance the struggle." He points out that after Marcos, the Aquino government redistributed the economy's surplus to a new set of cronies, relatives, lackeys, sycophants, and retainers. As he and other writers anticipated, it did not take long (less than two months) for the Aquino regime to "unsheathe the sword of war" against the people's movement.

*

Some notes are in order to clarify the task of the cultural worker in the national democratic struggle. It is illusory to believe that the alternative hegemony of the people's movement can be gained only through cultural or ideological work.

In 1988, the task of the cultural worker was spelled out at the founding of BUGKOS, an alliance of cultural workers, in a congress held in UP Diliman. The keynote speaker, a writer and academic, said that the primary concern of the cultural worker was to sever the psychic bond that ties the peasant to the landlord, or the worker to the factory owner of manager, out of a false consciousness manifested in the attitude of the dispossessed toward the padrone who has somehow provided them with the means of livelihood, however little they get out of it.

Once the bond is broken through a realization of their rights, the struggle then becomes a political one, and when fascist violence is applied against those struggling for social justice or economic rights one then begins to appreciate the meaning of self-defense. The cultural worker thus becomes involved not only in ideological struggle but also in political organizing and self-defense as well. Lines of work specializations are dissolved, and the cultural worker will require other than ideological (e.g. artistic or literary) skills. This is the reality of day-to-day cultural work in the countryside as well as in the cities.

The discourse or terms of reference of cultural and literary work may have changed somewhat since the 1970s but the essence of the conditions for conducting a protracted people's war continue to prevail: the hegemony of the United States and its surrogates in Philippine affairs; the unresolved land question; a ruling oligarchy or comprador class – a status quo that has bred poverty, criminality, corruption, exploitation, civil unrest, breakdown in basic social services, environmental destruction. Economic programs do not benefit the masses but the already privileged few.

The principles of *Talks at the Yenan Forum* are that "literature and art must fit well in the revolutionary machine and must operate as powerful weapons for uniting and educating the people and for attacking and destroying the enemy"; that literature must be a people's literature, not for the elite but for the masses, that people's literature is part of people's culture which is the alternative to ruling class culture or state-sponsored or –produced culture that passes for "popular culture"; that literature is produced by the people themselves, exercising their creativity to achieve freedom and regain their humanity.

Twenty-five years or so of literary theory and practice guided by these principles has produced a people's literature identified with the national democratic movement. The struggle for national democracy and socialism must stress the task of creating a "counterhegemonic" or what Antonio Gramsci calls a new integrated culture. Clearly antedating Gramsci (whose works became available in the Philippines in the 70s), Sison initiated the "Second Propaganda Movement" in the mid-60s. At about this time Renato Constantino articulated the need for "dissent and counterconsciousness." It was in the 60s that Mao Zedong's ideas on people's literature and art began to be assimilated by the radical youth.

For revolutionary writers the fusion of artistic and objective criteria simply means that to write well is more than a matter of style; it means honing the ideological and political tools that enable them to understand social realities. They thus serve not only as interpreters of people's experiences but are directly involved in changing social relations.

Filipino writers have discovered what a Third World writer said in 1959: "To take part in the African revolution, it is not enough to write a revolutionary song, you must fashion the revolution with the people. And if you fashion it with the people, the songs will come by themselves and of themselves."

At about that period Sison had already expressed his vision of a people's war in his poem "The Guerrilla Is Like a Poet." And being part of the Philippine revolution, the radical writer has learned to heed what Sison wrote in prison:

*Grasp well the bladed poem*
*And let it sing in your hands*
*This kampilan is a talisman*
*Of the people in red headbands.*

– Elmer Ordoñez*

---

* This article was originally written in 1993 and revised in 2009 for celebration the book publication in honor of Jose Maria Sison.

## Jose Maria Sison, Poet of the Proletariat

Jose Ma. Sison is alongside leaders of the proletariat like Mao Zedong and Ho Chi Minh who had a special interest in writing poetry. In the midst of practical leadership of the revolutionary movement, or all sorts of situations faced by a revolutionary in the performance of his tasks, they find time to express their thoughts about themselves, loved ones, society and revolution. This work is in addition to their recognition as individuals who stand for fundamental changes in their respective times and countries.

Among the poets like them, perhaps, Sison has the longest practice in writing poetry, up to five decades, from the 1950s as a student (AB English Literature) at the University of the Philippines to the present as a political refugee in the Netherlands, a status now in danger because of his being labelled by the United States and the European Union as "foreign terrorists." Consequently, the value of poetry has increased as a record of the major aspects of his life as a teacher and revolutionary, and the development of his poetry from the temporary phase of linguistic playing à la James Joyce ("By cokkis Lilly woundis") to the most simple summary of a very complex life of unremitting struggle ("In the Dark Depths," 94).

In a rare presentation of ars poetica, Sison said:

We assume here that to be mature and serious the poet has undergone a long and deepgoing process of arriving at a world outlook, enriching his life through personal experience and collective practice with others, mastering the language and learning from the literary masters and all along developing his own skills in the craft. But to create poems, the poet has to operate in the field of the poetic imagination constantly or at the least for extended periods of time.
– "Author's Note," in *Prison and Beyond: Selected Poems 1958–1983*, 11.

Here he is not far from depicting his own development as a poet/revolutionaty who may be emulated by others.

We know the place of poetry in the life of Sison, whatever happens, whatever is his situation in whichever place and time. In a poem, he says: "…the poems I compose are my ardent companions." ("Poems and Rest," 10 May 1978)

We also know that his poetry is located in the in life and struggle of the entire Filipino people.

– Gelacio Guillermo*

......
* First read during the "Evening of Salute to Professor Jose Ma. Sison" under the auspices of the College Editors Guild of the Philippines (CEGP), 14 November 2002, UP Faculty Center.

Nom de Guerre:
Tribute to Amado Guerrero (Jose Maria Sison)

"Bakit Amado Guerrero?" Ginunita ng Ambot,
Tulad ng elepanteng hindi nakalilimot
(Alam mo na, mula sa kantang may linyang
'Like an elephant, I'll never forget')
Pero hindi natuto makaraan ang apatnapung taon, ang iyong
                                                      alik-ik,
Na kakatwang sagot at di sagot: "Ang ibig sabihin niyon
Ay Beloved Warrior." Mandirigmang Minamahal.
Paano nga ba ipaliliwanag na sa ilalim
Ng pangalang iyan, na isang adhikang lagi't laging
Pinatutunayang nararapat, ay lalagumin mo ang kolektibong
                                                      kadalubhasaan
Ng Partido at ng mamamayan, at ang karanasan
Sa pakikibaka ng mga mamamayan
Sa ibang bahagi ng mundo; tuturulin mo
Ang ugat ng krisis sa ating lipunan
At ang pangangailangan para sa rebolusyon;
Ililinaw mo kung sino sa mga uring panlipunan
Ang kaibigan at kaaway, ang mga tungkulin
Ng rebolusyonaryong pwersa at masa,
Ang pamumuno sa organisasyon mula sa pinakamataas
Hanggang sa antas ng sangay sa bukid at pabrika,
Ang linyang pampulitika, ang istratehiya

At mga taktika ng matagalang digmang bayan
Sa pulupulo't bulubunduking bayan,
Ang sosyalistang perspektiba ng rebolusyon.
(Ngayong bagsak ang Wall Street,
Best seller ang Das Kapital!)
Kinakatawan ng Amado Guerrero ang teorya at praktika
Tungo sa pag-agaw ng kapangyarihang pulitikal
At pagbubuo ng bagong lipunan.
"Boring," anang Ambot. "You squeeze the life from learning
By focusing on theoretical frameworks and other boring stuff."
Ampaw.
May paliwanag si Lenin tungkol sa mga kasamang lider
Tulad ni Jose Ma. Sison–Amado Guerrero. Anya:

> *Natataranta sila [tinutukoy ang mga Ekonomista na inaakusahan ni Lenin ng pagtatanggol sa 'pagpapatihuli ng mga maalam na lider sa ispontanyong pagkamulat ng masa'] sa usapin ng ugnayan ng mga bahaging 'materyal' (ispontanyo...) at ideolohikal (maalam, kumikilos 'batay sa plano') ng kilusan. Hindi nila naiintindihan na ang 'ideolohista' ay karapat-dapat lamang sa gayong pagturing kung inuunahan niya ang ispontanyong kilusan, itinuturo ang landas, at may kakayahang manguna sa lahat sa paglutas ng lahat ng mga usaping teoretikal, pulitikal, taktikal at organisasyunal na ispontanyong sinasagupa ng mga 'bahaging materyal.' Para tunay na mabigyan ng 'pagsasaalang-alang ang mga bahaging ispontanyo ng kilusan,' kailangang kilanlin sila nang mahusay, kailangang ituro ang mga panganib at depekto ng ispontaneidad at itaas sa antas ng pagkaalam. Gayunman, sa pagsasabing*

> *hindi maibabaling ng mga ideolohista (i.e., mga lider na may kaalamang pulitikal) sa ibang landas ang kilusang pinagpapasyahan ng inter-aksyon ng kapaligiran at mga bahagi, binabale-wala ang simpleng katotohanang ang maalam na bahagi ay lumalahok sa inter-aksyong ito at sa pagpapasya ng landas.* – V. I. Lenin, "Pag-uusap sa mga tagapagtanggol ng ekonomismo," 1901.

Kahit ang Nicolai Lenin ay isa rin namang
Nom de guerre ni Vladimir Ilyich Ulyanov.
Bakit hindi nom de plume? Pustura lang iyan,
Tulad ng Doveglion ni Xose Garcia Villa
O ng Dandelion (halaman o ngipin ng leon?)
Ng tatay ng Hatsing Glue. Di tulad ng nom de guerre
Na tumitindig sa mga adhika ng rebolusyon:
Servando Magbanua, Elias del Pilar, Victoria Manalo,
Victor Bisperas, Pumuluyo Libre, Farra Tattao, Che Guevara,
Wayawaya, Bagani, Rosa Labrador, Marcial Macias,
Armando Liwanag. Bakit Armando Liwanag?
Ang ibig sabihin niyan ay Mandirigma ng Liwanag.
Mistulang pulang banderitang wumawagayway
Ang bawat pangalan: Liberacion Roja, Victor Rojo,
Jovencio Rojo Maglaya, Clarita Roja, Virginia Rojo,
Rio Rojo, Guia Roja, Ricardo Rojo, Roja Esperanza.
Aakalain ba ng kaaway na may pulang lihim
Ang Popoy Dakuykoy o ang Diosdado Calamidad,
O may subersibong akronim sa Bernardo R. Carpio?
Sa mga kolektib, ang pangalan sa pakikibaka
Ay panlansangan, na inuunahan ng Ka –

Bino, George, Ibay, Yokan, Sol, Vox, Ruth,
Boy, Poloy, Arting, Bagnos, Igme, Basyong,
Eid, Zippo, Sonya, Ting, Tingting.
Kapag uminit, karakang binabago, tulad ng kay
Cesar Lacara – Che, Rodel, Marcial, Lauro,
Jose, Roy, Tatang – sagisag na rin ng haba
Ng kanyang paglilingkod sa nayon at lungsod,
Sa lumang Partido at bagong Partido
Hanggang edad nobenta.
At nasaan na ngayon ang mga batang
Wala pang nom de guerre ay bininyagang
Lenin, Lenina, Mao, Maolen, Karl, Redsa,
Remnin Ribao, Andres (Bonifacio), Diego (Silang)?
May mga nom de guerre na nananatiling buhay
Sa kilusan. May mga nom de guerre
Na nawalan na ng saysay sa kilusan.
Marami ang nawalan ng Ka.
Mas marami ang sumasampa
Nanlalagim man ang kampanyang
DisarmamentDemobilizationRehabilitation ng rehimen.
Sa mga larangang gerilya, nakapangalan ang kumand
Sa tunay na pangalan ng mga bayani –
Si Venerando Villacillo ang Ka Bening,
Si Merardo Arce ang Dave, si Crispin Tagamolila
Ang Ka Cely, si Wilfredo Gacosta
Ang Geronimo Dulongtimog, si Chadli Molintas ang Chadli.
Pero hindi mo nalilimutang parangalan, Joema,
Ang mga kasamang kumilos nang tahimik,
Tulad ng aking estudyanteng si Antero Santos

Ng Ilocos, tulad ng aming si Tatang ng Tundo:
"Isang kasamang tahimik," sabi mo, "di makasarili
At walang humpay sa paggawa ang bumubuo
Sa katauhan ni Ka Che. Nasa kanya
Ang katangiang Komunista na gumawa
Para sa rebolusyon na mas madalas ay lingid
Kaysa yaong alam ng madla. Lubos
At makabuluhang nabuhay sa rebolusyonaryong
Pagsisilbi sa proletaryado at mamamayan."
Bakit Amado Guerrero? Sapagkat siya
Ang mandirigmang minamahal.
Hey, Joema, kanino nga bang nom de guerre
Itong Salvador del Mundo?
Ambot. Ampaw din?

— Gelacio Guillermo[*]

......
[*] From *Jose Maria Sison: A Celebration*, ed. The Production Group (Quezon City: Aklat ng Bayan, 2011), 58–62.

For Jose Ma. Sison and All Poet-Dreamers of the Revolution

One thinks of Jose Ma. Sison and of all poets in the struggle
As one imagines contradictions at every step,
Their minds constructing metaphors that break
The rules of the bourgeois and of the ruling class naturally

But because the rulers have appropriated Mother Nature
And Mother Earth and God's bounty to themselves
As if they could actually possess the earth, sky, and sea
And dispense every piece of them to every human life

At their will and from their imperialist machines;
Nature has become private estate of the greedy,
And the rest of common society, their slaves.
Through their robotic eyes, we see holographs

Of figures and animes in reconstructed spaces:
Trees with square tops, wildlife in artificial wilds
Landscapes and seascapes on canvasses that flutter
In the wind that was never wind but plugged-in blowers

And alas, perverted minds appearing brilliant
For having devised guns and planes and bombs

That pulverized people and all of life, blackened the air,
Destroyed Mother Earth and all of Mother Nature completely.

What a catastrophe, alas, how bereft of reason!
How lacking of heart and humanity, what insanity!
To begin with, the world had moved regardless
Of what men and women thought or did,

Winds blew, rains fell, the sun came and went,
Flowers bloomed, birds flew, seas got wedded to land,
Babies smiled at birth, parents loved and laughed
In perfect bliss, as there was harmony and there was peace

A progression, as of music, sustained life naturally:
The order breeding human kindness, friendships
Happy lives, loves and truths most real, freedom;
With no fall, no lag, no lines askew along fine points.

The thinker poet did not have to bleed to death
To sing and dream as the world moved quite painlessly;
The "falcon and the falconer"\* heard each other clearly
And plunder and slavery were never sins of nature.

But that was thousands and bloody thousands of years ago
Before money and property and capital reigned
Before Marx and Mao and all divined the entire game
Aeons before Joma wrote PSR and showed our life story.

......
\* The road stretches long and time could lose us / But songs of struggle will resound and freedom, won.

No, there may not be metaphors enough to signify,
Imperialist plunder, enslavement, and false minds,
No poem to render grief for murdered friends and dreamers
Yet hope and love for freedom grow far longer than all lifetimes.
One thinks of Joma, Karl, and Mao laid out on the same map
As with the rest of us, caught up in the dialectic
That once might not have been, but singing and dreaming
Anyhow, for what value is a life that knows no freedom?
What greater poem or song than that of revolution,
What is there most ennobling than service to the people,
What dream higher than soaring back to pure, untrammeled
                                                    nature
What cause more honest than that which keeps us whole?

To our dear comrade and friend, Professor Joma Sison, we give our thanks for the guidance and the inspiration

– Nonilon V. Queaño*

---

\* From *Jose Maria Sison: A Celebration*, ed. The Production Group (Quezon City: Aklat ng Bayan, 2011), 70–1.

## Patriot and Poet

I, LUIS V. TEODORO, of legal age, Filipino citizen, with postal address at College of Mass Communication, University of the Philippines, Diliman, Quezon City, after being duly sworn to in accordance with law, hereby depose and state: That –

1. I am a professor of journalism at the University of the Philippines (UP), Diliman, Quezon City. I was Dean of the College of Mass Communication of U.P. for two terms and am the highest ranking professor of the College, which has a complement of about 34 full-time faculty members, and 40 lecturers;

2. I have been a writer and journalism practitioner for more than 30 years. I am currently the Editor of the *Philippine Journalism Review*, a bimonthly publication that monitors the performance of the Philippine press in terms of accuracy, balance, fairness and contribution to the making of a well-informed citizenry; and of *Jounalism Asia*, an annual review which does the same thing on an Asia-wide basis and which is composed of journalists and academics from several countries of the region;

3. I am a columnist for the Manila newspaper *Today*, as well as for the online news service *abs-cbnnews.com*. In these columns, I comment on Philippine political developments as well as on the problems of Philippine society, culture,

and politics and governance. These publications may be accessed through the Internet for confirmation;

4. I have written a number of books, among them *Out of This Struggle: The Filipinos in Hawaii,* published by the University Press of Hawaii in 1982; *Two Views on Philippine Literature and Society* (with E. San Juan, Jr.), published in 1981 by the Center for Asian and Pacific Studies of the University of Hawaii; *The Summer of Our Discontent,* a collection of literary criticism published in 1987; *Mass Media Laws and Regulations in the Philippines* (with Rosalinda Kabatay), published by the Asian Media and Information Centre of Singapore in 1998 and 2001; *The Press and the Mass Media, Development and Democracy* (with Melinda de Jesus), published by the University of the Philippines' National College of Public Administration and Governance. A collection of my short fiction and literary criticism is under preparation, to be published by the University of the Philippines Press. I am also a writer of social realist fiction who has won several writing awards starting 1968.

5. I met Prof. Sison at the University of the Philippines' student newspaper the *Philippine Collegian* sometime in 1962, when I was a student and he was taking his masters' degree. Prof. Sison was Research Editor of that publication, while I was Features editor, and later, Literary Editor. I had the opportunity to read the articles written by Prof. Sison at the time, among them one called "Requiem for Lumumba," which described the assassination of that leader and patriot of the people of the Congo at the instigation of the US Central Intelligence Agency. This article was a turning point

in my political development; it revealed to me the reality of imperialism. Indeed it was not only the articles of Prof. Sison which had a profound influence on me as well as other staff members of the *Collegian,* but also his analysis of events in the Philippines at the time.

6. Because of my work experience in the *Collegian,* I was asked by Prof. Sison to edit the first edition of his work *Struggle for National Democracy,* a collection of his essays and speeches in which he analyzed Philippine social and political reality, and which has since become a classic every political activist in the Philippines has had occasion to read and learn from.

7. One cannot over-emphasize the impact of Prof. Sison's work and writing on Philippine society. His analysis of its problems is still one of the most incisive and relevant to have ever been written since the days of the Philippine Revolution of 1896, and his literary writings, consisting mostly of poetry as collected in *Selected Poems, The Guerilla Is Like a Poet,* and *Prison Poems* have been models for an entire generation of revolutionary poets.

8. In response to the reality of a country of grave injustice, vast poverty and deep social inequities, Prof. Sison proposed revolutionary solutions to achieving authentic independence and social revolution. He has many times asserted that this will not happen without a protracted struggle, and events have proven him right.

9. *The Philippine political elite has not hesitated to massacre entire communities, to arrest, detain and torture political and social activists, and to concoct such myths as that the revo-*

*lutionary movement and its leaders, specially Prof. Jose Ma. Sison, are terrorists.*

10. The inclusion of Prof. Sison – a writer, revolutionary and patriot – in any list of terrorists anywhere is totally unwarranted. I have never heard or read him as saying that the revolutionary movement, which owes its revival to his efforts in the 1960s and 1970s, should use terrorist methods. On the contrary, he has condemned such methods as counter-revolutionary and as totally alien to the values and goals of the revolutionary movement.

11. Unsubstantiated by the facts, the labeling of Prof. Sison as a terrorist is also politically motivated. The Philippine government initiated this labeling for the expressed purpose of "forcing the National Democratic Front to the negotiating table," as the Philippine Foreign Affairs Secretary has many times said in public.

12. The NDF has been steadfast in its commitment to peace talks. It is the Philippine government that has several times suspended them. When pressed for reasons, Philippine government spokespersons have said that the talks can only go on if the NDF laid down its arms, and is otherwise weakened through other means. The declaration of the New People's Army as a terrorist and of Prof. Jose Ma. Sison as a terrorist is one of these means. Through the inclusion of the NPA and Prof. Sison in the list of international terrorists, it hopes to weaken and intimidate the NDF enough to "force it to the negotiating table" under the government's terms.

13. The result of this politically motivated campaign has been to unjustly condemn Prof. Sison, who has many times con-

demned acts of terrorism, and who in fact condemned the September 11 attacks in the United States, as a terrorist himself.

14. The revolutionary movement with which Prof. Sison's name is indivisibly linked and of which he has been a leader and a continuing inspiration, is not a terrorist movement by a few conspirators who must use terrorist means for political ends.

15. This movement is supported by millions of Filipinos in the Philippines and abroad, as well as by men and women in other countries who correctly see the movement as a genuine response to the grave social injustice, mass poverty and disenfranchisement of the Filipino majority. It has established governments in many areas of the Philippines, and commands the respect and admiration of the Filipino masses who live in those areas, and the protection it provides them from criminal elements and other marauders.

16. This movement is the Filipino people's only hope for a change in the misery and brutality of their circumstances, which for hundreds of years have prevailed in the Philippines. The revolution the NDF and its allied organizations are fighting is a continuation of the Philippine Revolution thwarted by the United States at the turn of the century, when that Revolution had defeated Spanish colonial power and founded the first Asian Republic. While the Philippine Revolution was not the creation of Prof. Sison, his role in its resurgence makes him a patriot, not a terrorist.

17. I have known Prof.Sison for over thirty years, since his days as a faculty member of the Department of English

and Comparative Literature of the University of the Philippines. In all those years I have known him he has steadfastly upheld the rights of the Filipino people, whom he regards as his sovereign.

18. I have also had occasion to listen to him speak and to read his writings, many of which condemn the use of tactics such as that proposed by Simoun, a character in our national hero Jose Rizal's novel *Noli Me Tangere,* of worsening the social crisis by contributing to the people's misery. I have read and heard him condemn any act that targets civilians and non-combatants. Terrorism by definition targets ordinary people and non-combatants. It is inconceivable for someone who has committed all his life to the service of the Filipino masses to treat their lives as cavalierly as terrorists do.

19. While Prof. Sison's contributions to the Filipino people's revolution are undisputed, Prof. Sison is also a poet whose writing and views on literature have taught and inspired two generations of Filipino writers, including myself and literally hundreds of others.

20. His political thoughts have had the same influence. Since he began writing on Philippine politics more than three decades ago, Prof. Sison has provided thousands upon thousands of Filipinos a framework for the analysis of the political structures of the Philippines, and thousands upon thousands of activists involved in changing Philippine society an indispensable means for understanding the interplay between Philippines social relations, politics and culture.

21. Just as I regard his collections of poetry as valuable contributions to the development of Philippine literature, I regard his political writings as equally important to the development of Philippine political thought since the Revolutionary period when, in the course of the struggle against Spanish rule such Filipinos as Jose Rizal and Apolinario Mabini examined the realities of Philippine politics and its role in the making of a just society.
22. To label a patriot, political thinker, and poet such as Prof. Sison a terrorist is therefore a gross injustice driven by the narrowest political motives.

IN WITNESS WHEREOF, I have hereunto affixed my signature this 10th day July 2003 at Makati, Philippines.

(sgd.) LUIS V. TEODORO Affiant

SUBSCRIBED AND SWORN to before me this 10th day of July 2003 at Makati City, Philippines. Affiant Luis V. Teodoro exhibited to me his Community Tax Certificate No. 18742227, issued on January 16, 2003 at Antipolo City.

Doc. No. 54; Page No. 12; Book No. II; Series of 2003.

## Jose Maria Sison as Poet

The best-known radical poet who became a political prisoner of the Marcos regime was Jose Ma. Sison, a former English instructor at the University of the Philippines, who spent ten years in prison, and wrote a whole volume of poems (much later set to music out of which a CD would be made) which spoke not only of his privations during his incarceration, but of his steadfast political views. Sison was arguably the most important political prisoner under martial law, for he was the chairman of the reestablished Communist Party of the Philippines. After years spearheading the radical movement in the Philippines since his university days, he would seal his place in Philippine history as the moving spirit behind the Marx- and Mao-inspired movement that has always been described as the "longest-running communist insurgency in the world."

While still behind bars, his friends in academe and fellow writers put together his poems and published them in a book, *Prison and Beyond*. One of the pieces in this collection speak of the prisoner's faith in the power of his writings, and of his certainty that outside his prison cell, the struggle which he helped launch continues.

Poems and Rest

*Since a long, long time ago*
*Incantations and prayers*
*Have been a comfort*
*To those who suffer.*

*Lying down at night,*
*I recite my poems*
*Until my throat runs dry*
*And I fall asleep in comfort.*

*But my poems are different.*
*They appeal to the people.*
*I put my trust in them*
*And in their firm struggle.*

*While at rest I am sure*
*That the struggle goes on.*
*And when my rest is over*
*I will do what I can.*

*Solitary confinement*
*Is torture so vicious.*
*But the poems I compose*
*Are my ardent companions.*

– Jose Maria Sison, *Prison and Beyond*, 80.

Years after his release from prison, and while already living in exile in the Netherlands, Sison was interviewed by a graduate student at De La Salle University for her master's thesis. Among other things, he was asked about the role of literature in the protest movement against martial law.

How important was protest literature during the Martial Law years, especially those written by members of the party?

Protest literature in English, Pilipino and various other Philippine languages were exceedingly important during the martial law years. The biggest amount of revolutionary literature, in the form of poetry, lyrics for songs, short stories, plays and some novels, was written by communists and revolutionary mass activists.

The creative works were carried by national and regional underground publications of the revolutionary movement. In urban areas, poems were recited and performed in lightning mass actions and in large mass actions, especially from 1979 onwards. In all the years of martial rule, the revolutionaries produced and performed creative works in the guerrilla fronts.

How effective was it in fighting the dictatorship?

The protest literature was very effective in fighting the dictatorship. Poems and lyrics of songs could circulate most easily. They were inspiring and they could circulate fast and nationwide, with the help of underground revolutionary organizations, including cultural organizations. They were so much easier to circulate than political tracts and much more easily understood by the masses.

The enemy had no effective way of stopping these. Without the protest literature, the revolutionary movement would have been drab and dull. But with protest literature, it became lively and militant. The protest literature was effective in spreading the revolutionary message because it could move instantly the hearts and minds of the people. The message reached the masses in a form that they could easily grasp.

The Life and Times of a Seditious Poet
(A Poem on Jose Maria Sison)


Not for him the contemplation of coconuts,
virgin or otherwise, succulent to tongue and teeth,
but the bitter crop of tales from his country
of broken peasants and rebel hunters.
Not for him pink raisins but the rose
that bleeds in thriving on thorny bush
not for him blue monks but the bluer
mounts standing sentry to the plains.
He still dreams of the pole star to the north,
a lantern that lit up his path through forests
and fields, but as the world turns, celestials
happen to spin off in their own selfish orbits
and it's come to pass the old dragon gods
make monkeys out of us, they fiddle up
their island lackeys who have grown fat
from the barrel, the larder and the vat.
In far exile, his poems and hymns still excite
trilling like bird song, moving like the wind
stirring up old ashes of departure, the phoenix
if you will, and in our sleep, we hear him sing:
"Ay! we'll line them up against the righteous wall
draw blood from their soul if they have one at all

and the millions will rise above this weary pall
of feudal order, the peace of a gray eternal fall."

– Ed Maranan*

......
* First published in the UP Institute of Creative Writing's *LIKHAAN* literary journal, Vol. 3, 2009.

Contents

Foreword ..... 5
Preface ..... 17

*first part · the people's resistance*
*unang bahagi · ang paglaban ng sambayanan*

The Guerrilla Is Like a Poet ..... 24
  Ang Gerilya'y Tulad ng Makata ..... 25
The Bladed Poem ..... 28
  Ang Tulang may Talim ..... 29
The Woman and the Strange Eagle ..... 32
  Ang Babae at ang Dayong Agila ..... 33
Against the Monster on the Land ..... 36
  Laban sa Halimaw sa Lupa ..... 37
The Forest Is Still Enchanted ..... 40
  Nakakabighani Pa ang Gubat ..... 41
Defy the Reptile ..... 42
  Labanan ang Buwaya ..... 43
The Central Plains ..... 46
  Ang Gitnang Kapatagan ..... 47
From a Burning Bush ..... 48
  Mula sa Umaapoy na Palumpong ..... 49
The Coming of the Rain ..... 50
  Ang Pagdating ng Ulan ..... 51

| | |
|---|---|
| Under the Rain | 52 |
|   Sa Ulan | 53 |
| Rain and Sun on the Mountains | 54 |
|   Ulan at Araw sa Kabundukan | 55 |
| The North Star Is Always There | 58 |
|   Laging Naroon ang Hilagang Tala | 59 |
| In Praise of Martyrs | 60 |
|   Papuri sa mga Martir | 61 |
| Wisdom from a Comrade | 62 |
|   Dunong Mula sa isang Kasama | 63 |
| What Makes a Hero | 64 |
|   Ang Pagiging Bayani | 65 |

*second part · detention and defiance*
*ikalawang bahagi · pagkapiit at paglaban*

| | |
|---|---|
| Fragments of a Nightmare | 68 |
|   Mga Piraso ng Bangungot | 69 |
| In the Dark Depths | 94 |
|   Sa Madilim na Kailaliman | 95 |
| Pearl | 96 |
|   Perlas | 97 |
| Gold | 98 |
|   Ginto | 99 |
| Chemistry of Tears | 100 |
|   Kimika ng Luha | 101 |
| A Furnace | 102 |
|   Pugon | 103 |

| | |
|---|---:|
| A Cool Breeze | 104 |
|    Sariwang Simoy | 105 |
| Like a Giant, Like a Bird | 106 |
|    Tulad ng Higante, Tulad ng Ibon | 107 |
| My Poems Are Militant | 110 |
|    Militante ang mga Tula Ko | 111 |
| I Am Determined To Rise | 112 |
|    May Pasya Akong Bumangon | 113 |
| My Spiritual Weapon | 114 |
|    Ang Aking Sandatang Pandiwa | 115 |
| Nothing More Beautiful | 120 |
|    Walang Mas Maganda | 121 |
| I Am Always with You | 122 |
|    Lagi Ko Kayong Kasama | 123 |
| You Are My Wife and Comrade | 126 |
|    Asawa Kita at Kasama | 127 |
| Across Blue Waters | 130 |
|    Sa Ibayong Dagat na Asul | 131 |
| To Jasm, My Captive Child | 134 |
|    Kay Jasm, Anak Ko sa Piitan | 135 |

*third part · the struggle continues*
*ikatlong bahagi · patuloy ang pakikibaka*

| | |
|---|---:|
| Sometimes, the Heart Yearns for Mangoes | 140 |
|    Minsa'y Sabik ang Puso sa Mangga | 141 |
| The Giant Oak | |
| (Tribute to Comrade Mao Zedong) | 144 |

| | |
|---|---:|
| Ang Higanteng Roble (Parangal kay Kasamang Mao Zedong) | 145 |
| Monsters in the Market (Song Lyrics) | 148 |
| Mga Halimaw sa Pamilihan (Titik Awit) | 149 |
| The Way to a Just Peace (Song Lyrics) | 152 |
| Ang Daan sa Makatarungang Kapayapaan (Titik-Awit) | 153 |
| The Charge against Me | 156 |
| Ang Paratang sa Akin | 157 |
| Once More Solitary Confinement | 160 |
| Bartolina Muli | 161 |
| Cry for Freedom | 164 |
| Isigaw ang Kalayaan | 165 |
| The Inquisition | 168 |
| Ang Ingkisisyon | 169 |
| Demons in Two Domains | 172 |
| Mga Demonyo sa Dalawang Dominyo | 173 |
| My Pen and My Tongue | 176 |
| Aking Panulat at Dila | 177 |
| Rulers and Butchers | 180 |
| Mga Naghahari at Mangangatay | 181 |
| Stages of My Life | 184 |
| Mga Yugto Ng Buhay Ko | 185 |
| How Filipinos Forget the Unforgiveable | 186 |
| Paano Nalilimutan ng mga Pilipino ang Di-Mapapatawad | 187 |
| The Master Puppeteer and the Puppets | 190 |
| Ang Maestro ng Titiretero at mga Papet | 191 |

| | |
|---|---|
| The Monster Ravages the Forests and Mountains | 194 |
|     Sinasalanta ng Halimaw ang mga Gubat at Bundok | 195 |
| US Is the Terrorist Monster | 198 |
|     US ang Teroristang Halimaw | 199 |
| The Bells of Balangiga | 200 |
|     Mga Batingaw ng Balangiga | 201 |
| Tribute to Comrade Andres Bonifacio | 204 |
|     Parangal Kay Ka Andres Bonifacio | 205 |

## *fourth part · commentaries*

| | |
|---|---|
| Literary Craft and Commitment | 213 |
| Beyond Transcendence, Toward Incarnation: The Poetry of Jose Ma. Sison | 220 |
| Beyond Autobiography | 232 |
| Politics and Faith | 238 |
| From Literature to Revolution | 243 |
| The Legacy of Mao and Sison in People's Literature | 254 |
| Jose Maria Sison, Poet of the Proletariat | 264 |
| Nom de Guerre: Tribute to Amado Guerrero (Jose Maria Sison) | 266 |
| For Jose Ma. Sison and All Poet-Dreamers of the Revolution | 271 |
| Patriot and Poet | 274 |
| Jose Maria Sison as Poet | 281 |
| The Life and Times of a Seditious Poet (A Poem on Jose Maria Sison) | 285 |

www.ingramcontent.com/pod-product-compliance
Lightning Source LLC
Chambersburg PA
CBHW031423150426
43191CB00006B/371